HEALING

—— of ——

THE SOUL

VASILY TOKAREV

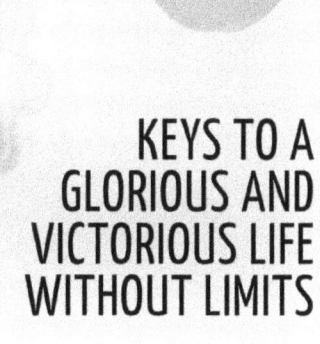

KEYS TO A GLORIOUS AND VICTORIOUS LIFE WITHOUT LIMITS

Baruch

Kyiv • 2016

CITIOFBOOKS, INC.
3736 Eubank NE Suite A1
Albuquerque, NM 87111-3579
www.citiofbooks.com
Hotline: 1 (877) 389-2759
Fax: 1 (505) 930-7244

Ordering Information:
Quantity sales. Special discounts are available on quantity purchases by corporations, associations, and others. For details, contact the publisher at the address above.

Printed in the United States of America.

ISBN-13:	Softcover	979-8-89391-099-5
	eBook	979-8-89391-100-8

Library of Congress Control Number: 2024909039

Acknowledgments

First and foremost, I'd like to thank my dear wife, Tanya, who has always been by my side and has been my support in all the years of my pastoral ministry. Thank you, dear, for your love, generosity, and understanding. You helped me go through crises in my own personal life and later helped bring inner healing to multitudes of God's children.

I am very grateful to my children: Vyacheslav, Aleksandr, Victor, Vladimir, Olga, and Mark. I thank you, precious ones, that with me, you went through all the difficulties that were associated with my ministry and my frequent absence from home. I can only partly understand you and how complicated it can be to be the child of a pastor, particularly when being subject to the highest demands and standards.

I am grateful to my dear daughter, Olga. Thank you, my sweetheart, for performing a colossal work and, in spite of your huge workload and busyness from attending a university, translating this book into the English language.

I am sincerely grateful to our Inner Healing Ministry team. Thank you, brothers and sisters, for responding to God's call and dedicating a mass of personal time for the service of spiritually wounded people. Thank you for being willing to let me go on ministry trips and consequently taking upon yourselves the burden and responsibility of ministry in our local church.

And the most tremendous gratitude goes to my Lord, Jesus. Thank You, Jesus, for taking my place on the cross of Calvary and for covering all the needs of my soul and fulfilling them through Your suffering. Thank You for healing my wounded heart and allowing me to be a witness of what You did and continue to do in the lives of my dear brothers and sisters. This book is written in Your name, Jesus, so that thousands of Your children could take advantage of all that You paid for with Your blood, suffering, and death on the shameful cross. Dear Jesus, all glory goes only to You!

Dedication

I would like to dedicate this book to all the brave and sincere children of God who wish to enter into the fullness of God's salvation and God's promises—to those who are not satisfied with just the crumbs of God's grace but wish to walk in the fire of the Holy Spirit.

This book is for those who are not afraid to honestly look in to their hearts, deal with their pasts, and finally take pleasure in the freedom of Christ in all the areas of their lives.

This book is for those who do not wish to blame others for their own weaknesses and failures but are ready to take upon themselves the responsibility for their relationships with God, their spiritual growth, and the fulfillment of God's will on this earth.

It is for those who are willing to forgive their offenders, those willing to be freed from all bondage, and those willing to destroy every curse and demonic control over themselves.

This book is for those who want to know who they are in Jesus Christ, what a glorious inheritance they have, and what a limitless and omnipotent God dwells in them.

Allow the Holy Spirit to take you by the hand and move you step-by-step from a negative past and present into a glorious future.

Contents

CHAPTER 1

Pain of the Soul

There are numerous similarities between the human soul and the physical body. When the physical body is healthy, functioning correctly, and is not subject to any negative influence from the outside, it is free from all pain. Physical pain is an indicator of possible irregularities within the body, and pain in the soul works similarly. Pain suggests that the soul is unwell and that something is not right with it.

If the soul is in pain, then there is always a reason for it because the soul is the spiritual part of each person. To make sense of the soul, and to find a way out of our existing problems, it is necessary to turn to the origins of human life.

The existence of humanity is not an accidental occurrence, and it is not the result of an explosion in space. Humans are the most unique creation in the entire universe, and God created us in His own image and likeness to rule over the earth. We were created to have free and happy lives, and God did not plan our destiny to be bound for misery, disease, and death. All the negative things that people have to deal with today were the result of the wrong choices of Adam, the first man on earth.

Being deceived by the Devil, this man rejected the dominion of a loving God over himself. Because of this, by default, the rest of humankind fell under the dominion of the Enemy of God—and we became his slaves. This rebellion and sin toward God led to troubles such as disease, misery, sadness, suffering, loneliness, and death in the life of humanity. There is not one single person on this earth who is present without sin. Similar to inherited cancer cells, it is born with us. By satisfying the unholy desires within ourselves, humankind became a slave to its own sin.

Just like cancer is a foreign organism in the body of an individual, so is sin a foreign spiritual organism in the soul of an individual as well. As cancer grows, it interferes with the normal functioning of the human body. As sin grows, it too interferes with the wellness and best qualities of the human soul.

It is sin that became the cause of all spiritual pain and wounds. We either inflict suffering on ourselves by sinning, or others inflict this pain on us by sinning even if we don't. Humanity became part of a vicious cycle, and we began to hurt ourselves and one another. There is not one person who has not hurt someone before, just as there is not one person who has not been hurt by someone else. This very earthly life, similar to people, is saturated with sin and curse, and in turn, that brings humankind a lot of suffering.

The Violin

There once lived a famous violinist who performed concerts by playing on violins that he had made with his own bare hands. He had one violin that he especially loved. While cutting out its shape, he put all his craftsmanship and effort into that one violin. It differed from all the other ones because it gave out especially gentle sounds. The master treasured this violin, and he valued it very much; while playing on it, he achieved tremendous popularity and fame.

This violinist also had one enemy who envied him and always tried to sabotage him in some way. Seeing that he could not do anything to the violinist himself, the enemy stole the master's beloved violin. After holding on to it for a little while, he sold it for a very high price.

The violin then began its journey through many places. It was used in concert halls and in various clubs, bars, and restaurants. It went through many hands after being sold at auctions and various markets. It was treated very carelessly, and most times it ended up underneath the feet of playing children.

Many years passed, and the violin lost its former beauty. It ceased to sound as captivating as it once had in the hands of its former owner. No one treated it as tenderly and with as much love as he had. Finally, covered in dust and with few strings left, a tattered bow, and deep scratches on its body, it found itself in a large hall among cheap articles being readied for auction.

The auctioneer, after one glance at the old and tattered violin and not finding any value in it, asked for three dollars. It was fairly noisy in the hall, and nobody was interested in the old violin. Suddenly, from the back rows stood up an old and graying man. With quick footsteps, he walked up to the auctioneer and took the violin into his trembling hands. For a couple of moments, the man intently studied the violin. Finally, he dusted it off, straightened out the bow, tightened the few strings that were left, and gently propped it up against his chest. The bow slid across the strings, and an unearthly melody filled the hall.

The hall was instantly transformed with silence. Leaving aside their conversations, and amazed at the captivating melody, the buyers suddenly felt as if they were at the concert of a renowned violinist. The violin found itself in the hands of its creator and owner. As soon as the last sounds died away, many hands were raised instantaneously. There were many who desired to buy the violin, and the violin was sold for $3,000.

The lives of many people are similar to the fate of the old violin. We live in a world where there is a lot of pain, misery, and tears. Suffering, betrayal, and ridicule have left deep wounds in the souls of men and women. Despite living among a busy society, people often feel themselves to be useless and alone.

All people dream of happy lives, wish one another this happiness, and spend their entire lives in pursuit of it. But this joy tends to stay far away and seems unattainable. Sometimes they feel as if they are so close, and they reach for it, but once again it slips right through their fingers.

Some people, however, don't give up and instead hope for success. They try to create good family atmospheres, study for prestigious professions, earn a lot of money, raise their children, and prepare for old age. But oftentimes, finally, after exhausting lives, in their hearts they discover absolute emptiness, loneliness, and harsh disappointment.

Others, after not seeing a purpose for life, treat it as if it has no value. They destroy themselves through various unhealthy habits and negative lifestyles. It doesn't matter to them when or how their lives end. They are not interested in who their children will one day become or what their descendants will say about them in the future.

Finally, the third group of people, discouraged in life and not having found in it any value, end their lives, leaving behind brokenhearted loved ones and deeply wounded close friends.

Only when the life of a person is touched by Him who created it can this person be able to find genuine happiness, purpose, and true value. When each person allows his or her Creator to touch his or her wounded soul, take away all the pain, and heal all his or her wounds, then in each person's heart a new melody of love, freedom, and happiness is born. These people are then able to feel truly loved, and they acquire the ability to love as well.

God, our Lord and Creator, really loves each person on this earth. He has created a blessed destiny and wonderful plan for each of our lives. When we allow Him to come into our lives and bring order and restoration, our lives are completely transformed. The pain leaves, depression disappears, and all bitterness, discouragement, confusion, hate, and anxiety goes away. We acquire a loving, heavenly Father who is able to do all things, and our hearts find true freedom.

It's similar to the story of the eaglet.

The Eaglet

Once a farmer found an eagle's nest with one single egg still inside. Upon coming home, he put the egg under a sitting hen to see what would happen, and in time, a young eaglet hatched out of the egg. Living on the farm among the chickens, the eaglet learned all of the chickens' mannerisms and ate their feed. He even learned to dig through manure and to look for worms. But sometimes, on days of celebration, the farmer would toss him pieces of meat.

The more the eaglet grew, the more he was convinced that he greatly differed from his "relatives." His nose was too crooked and sharp; his feet grew strong claws—and his eyes! His gaze was penetrating, and it was oriented somewhere far away. He always wanted to know what existed beyond the fence—things that his fellow chickens hardly ever bothered to dwell on.

After a significant amount of time passed, the eaglet began to feel uncomfortable in the henhouse. He grew to hate chicken feed and the smell of manure, and he grew bored with the games of his friends. The eaglet longed for something else, but what that was he himself hardly knew. Subconsciously, he understood that something was not right. The farm was like a prison to him, and life was empty and boring. Discouragement and emptiness began to grip his eagle heart more and more often. He considered himself completely alone among the happy chickens.

One fall day, when dark storm clouds loomed in the sky, an eagle appeared over the farm. He soared freely, straightening out his mighty and broad wings. Suddenly, far below, on a dirty farm and among the busy chickens, the soaring eagle saw something dear and familiar. In the yard among the birds stood the now matured eaglet, with head lowered and folded wings.

After circling in the sky a couple of times, the eagle flew down and let out a screech to attract the attention of the young eaglet. Hearing the penetrating cry from the sky, the chickens, overtaken with fear, darted to the henhouse. Only the eaglet stood frozen in place. In that eagle cry he heard something dear, familiar, and heartfelt. For the first time in his life, he lifted up his head to look into the heavens. Against the background of storm clouds, he saw an eagle soaring freely and majestically. His heart began to quicken, for in the soaring bird, he something akin to himself.

Lowering his head, the eagle looked at himself. Then he looked upward again, again at himself, and again at the sky. He suddenly began to understand something. Straightening out his wings, he tried to take off, but at first, he did not succeed. It appeared as though his own wings did not want to obey his mind.

Again, the eagle's cry sounded from the sky, calling him upward. The eaglet began to wave his wings, trying to take off from the ground, which, like a strong magnet, did not want to let him go. However, the wave of his wings got stronger and stronger, and suddenly, a strong gust of wing grabbed ahold of the despondent eaglet and began to lift him higher and higher, drawing him into the endless span of the skies.

While drawing ever closer to the skies, slightly waving with his big wings, and directing them under the currents of air, the eaglet finally felt a taste of true freedom. Finally, he had obtained that which his eagle heart had longed for all his life.

After making a circle above the henhouse, the two free birds, having pierced the dark storm clouds, flew even higher into the heavens and began to play by coming in and out of the sun's setting rays.

When living among a noisy and, at first glance, exciting crowd, people often feel themselves lonely and useless.

Somewhere deep within, they are longing for a true and selfless love, faithful friendships, and normal human relationships. They desire something pure and holy.

A human soul may find the answer to its questions and needs only when, surrounded by faith, he or she is able to experience a true encounter with his or her Creator.

CHAPTER 2

Encounter with God

The Bible contains many examples of people who had a personal encounter with God. Their experiences were never without impact; they always left indelible impressions on these people's lives. A person cannot remain the same after a personal encounter with God. Such an encounter leads a person to a place of decision, which then determines his or her future.

Isaiah was a great prophet in Israel. He was chosen by God and had already fulfilled his calling. He prophesied of the judgment and the punishment of God that awaited sinners and those who were dishonest. His prophetic predictions were addressed to different peoples and nations, as we read in the first five chapters of his book. In the sixth chapter, the great prophet experienced a personal type of revelation he had never experienced before. Isaiah suddenly saw God on a high and exalted throne. He was surrounded by seraphim, who, hiding their faces from God's glory, unceasingly exclaimed, "Holy, Holy, Holy is the Lord of Hosts; the whole earth is full of His glory!" (Isa. 6:3).

The doorposts shook with their exclamations, and the whole place was filled with smoke. What Isaiah saw moved him so much that he said, "Whoa is me, for I am undone! Because I am a man of unclean lips, and I dwell in the midst of a people of unclean lips: for my eyes have seen the King, the Lord of Hosts" (Isa. 6:5).

Only after the prophet was cleansed did he hear the word of the inquiring God: "Whom shall I send, and who will go for Us?" (Isa. 6:8).

With great confidence, Isaiah then answered, "Here am I. Send me."

After this experience, Isaiah became a new man and a great prophet. In exact detail he described the future suffering of Jesus Christ and the essence of His deeds. In spite of the difficulties that Isaiah faced, he was bold in the proclamation of God's truth.

The same could be said of Moses. He knew of his calling and purpose, but after escaping from Egypt, he lost all hope that his calling had ever existed. There was a time when he desperately wanted to help his brethren, but they did not understand him. During that time he had strength and position, but now all he had was a staff in his hand, sad memories, and with these, he humbly carried on with his life.

One day in the desert, Moses met God in a burning thornbush. God spoke to him and addressed the painful questions that Moses had struggled with from the earliest days of his understanding. The former events of Moses's life were so clear in his memory that it seemed to him as though they had happened just yesterday. Moses spoke with the one who could do things that he could only dream of. Once again, his life took on meaning. God sent Moses back to Egypt as a completely new man. He returned intending to leave again, but this time he didn't leave alone—he was with an army of three million strong men. This meeting in the desert made Moses a great leader, and God used him to miraculously deliver Israel from Egyptian slavery.

Another well-known man of God is Jacob. The name "Jacob" means "cunning one or deceiver." Jacob lived with this name for almost ninety-seven years. In practice, Jacob's name didn't suit him too badly. He managed to obtain the birthright of his brother by deceiving his father. Changing his clothes and calling himself by his brother's name, Esau, he received the blessing due to each firstborn son. Afraid of his brother's wrath, he fled his parents' home and set out for his uncle's home in search of a bride. In spite of all this, God was with him. His uncle Laban turned out to be just like Jacob—cunning and sly. Nevertheless, Jacob managed to deceive even him in return.

Twenty years later, Jacob returned home with his wives and great riches. When Esau heard that Jacob was coming, he came out to meet Jacob with four hundred men. Jacob understood that cunning and lies would not help him now. After sending his brother many gifts, Jacob found a place to be alone and began to seek God. He understood that only God could help him out of this situation. God had waited for this meeting for ninety-seven years, and finally it had come. Jacob needed help, and God needed Jacob, but God didn't need the old Jacob, He needed a new one. That night, Jacob took hold of God and would not let Him go until dawn. Finally, God began to speak. He asked, "What is your name?" "Jacob," came the answer. Jacob was brought to acknowledge his character as a liar and deceiver, which he hated to confess. When he finally laid down his old identity, he heard the words that changed his entire life: "Your name shall no longer be called Jacob, but Israel: for you have struggled with God and with men, and have prevailed" (Gen. 32:28).

Before He changed Jacob's image, God changed his name. For the remainder of his life, Jacob lived in accordance with this new name. When he moved to Egypt, even Pharaoh bowed before him as a hero of God.

One of the heroes of the New Testament was named Paul, but in the past, he had been called Saul. He was zealous for the law, tradition, and ancestral teachings. Fervent for God's work and righteous teaching, he persecuted the Church of Jesus Christ and was ready to give his life to wipe out Christian heresy. He tried to follow what he had been taught and admonished in from his childhood, confident that he was defending God's truth. Instead, it turned out that he was fighting against that very truth. He arrested Christians and dragged them into court, and this continued until he had an encounter with God. This encounter was a true collision with the truth that Saul had rejected, and with Jesus, whom he had persecuted. On the road to Damascus, a very bright light from heaven struck Saul. Blinded, he fell to the earth and heard a stern voice say, "Saul, Saul, why are you persecuting me?" Jesus was speaking to him. This meeting was so staggering that of the former proud Pharisee nothing remained. He became a great apostle of God and a preacher of the gospel, a message for which he lived and died.

God Himself orchestrated all of these meetings, and that's why many people expect similar miracles, hoping that God will supernaturally appear, and everything in their lives will suddenly be changed. Sometimes you will hear believers say, "If God wishes, then He will save me, heal me, bless me, baptize me in the Holy Spirit, and set me free." These people live all their lives passively waiting for something dramatic to happen, but this type of expectation is just another form of the Devil's deception.

Closed Door

One of the last phrases that Christ said as He hung on the cross was, "It is finished." With these words, Jesus accomplished absolutely everything necessary for humankind's salvation, healing, deliverance, and fulfillment of all needs. God already did all that He could do and already gave all that He could give. "That is, that God was in

Christ, reconciling the world to Himself, not imputing their trespasses to them; and has committed to us the word of reconciliation" (2 Cor. 5:19).

Here it speaks of a fact. God in Christ was reconciled with sinners. Further, the apostle Paul continues: "Now then, we are ambassadors for Christ, as though God were pleading through us: we implore you on Christ's behalf, be reconciled to God" (2 Cor. 5:20).

This Scripture shows us that reconciliation involves participation from both sides. God has already reconciled Himself to us, and now humankind must also reconcile in return. When an individual comes to God in full repentance, reconciliation begins. All of the fullness in the sacrifice of Jesus Christ belongs to everyone who lives on this earth. All that people need to do now is to receive this sacrifice into their lives by faith.

"And from the days of John the Baptist until now the kingdom of heaven suffers violence, and the violent take it by force" (Matt. 11:12). In this verse, Jesus is saying that in God's kingdom, nothing happens automatically. A person must make an effort to seek the kingdom of God.

The book of Revelation clearly illustrates what a person should do: "Behold, I stand at the door and knock. If anyone hears My voice and opens the door, I will come in to him, and dine with him, and he with Me" (Rev. 3:20).

Jesus stands at the closed door and knocks. He patiently waits for someone to open it. He desires to come and share supper with the one who is behind the closed door. Maybe that person is calling out to God for help, and as that person calls out, God knocks. In these situations, the Devil tries to come in and lie to the one who is praying to God, so he says, "God doesn't hear you. He doesn't love you, He forgot about you, and doesn't care about you or your problems. All of your prayers are in vain."

If you read carefully, you will notice that this verse mentions one significant detail—the door. Jesus waits and hopes that the one behind the door will one day hear His knock, open the door, and allow Him to come in. Individuals themselves must open the door to their hearts.

God wants to meet with us more than we want to meet with God. God wants to save sinners more than sinners want to be saved. God wants to heal the sick more than the sick want to be healed. Why is this? Firstly, because a sinner doesn't fully comprehend what he or she has lost by living by earthly standards or what terrible retribution awaits after death. Secondly, God knows that He has already paid the biggest price for all of humankind's needs—the sacrifice of His only begotten Son, Jesus Christ.

Unrecognized Messiah

This picture was similar to the time that Jesus Christ was on earth. The priesthood and all the people of Israel, congregating in the temple, prayed to God and asked Him to send them the Messiah. They cried and sincerely asked for deliverance. They told God how difficult it was for them, in what shame and oppression they lived, and how terribly tired they were of waiting for the Savior. At that same very moment, in the courtyard of the temple stood Jesus—the Savior and Messiah of Israel—and proclaimed, "If anyone thirsts, let him come to Me and drink ... Come to Me, all you who labor and are heavy laden, and I will give you rest" (John 7:37; Matt. 11:28).

Jesus called people to Himself for three and a half years. At the very same time, the people "sought" Him. To great misfortune, Jesus and the people didn't meet. Why didn't they meet?

Before Jesus came, God sent John the Baptist so that John could prepare the way for Jesus. The people of Israel had fallen far from God in their traditions and legends. People's hearts were hardened, their spiritual eyes blinded, and their ears deaf. The sin that lived inside of them separated them from God and made them hard-hearted. By preaching repentance and confession, John the Baptist played a necessary role in returning these people back to life. The first people who came to him were sinners, wanderers, thieves, alcoholics, and drug addicts. They were not confused by his outward appearance, and they were not upset with what he ate. It didn't bother them that his teaching wasn't taking place in the temple, but out in the desert instead. The people had only one desire—to be set free from their sinful burdens, and through the confession of their sins and sincere repentance, to be reconciled to God. "And when all the people heard Him, and the tax collectors justified God, having been baptized with the baptism of John. But the Pharisees and lawyers rejected the will of God for themselves, not having been baptized by him" (Luke 7:29–30).

The scribes and Pharisees used many arguments to avoid being baptized by John, but their biggest reason was that they didn't want to acknowledge their own horrible, sinful condition. They were good at pointing out all the sin in those around them, but they couldn't see the sin in their own lives. That's why when the Messiah, the One for whom they'd been praying and waiting for, had finally come, they didn't know Him. Unrepented sin did not allow them to recognize the Messiah. Only those with clear eyes, clean hearts, and true visions of themselves were able to see God.

Raising the Dam

God, as a loving Father, did absolutely everything required for the salvation of people through the sacrifice of Jesus Christ.

On the cross of Calvary, Jesus perfected salvation once and forever for all nations and all generations. Our heavenly Father paid a high price for our salvation, and He desires that all possess this salvation. He has so much good reserved for those who fear and love Him. The Bible says that God's love is beyond human understanding. Nevertheless, He wants us to know this love, to be filled with it, and to abide in it.

Allow me to use a small example. In the city where I spent my childhood, there was a dam covering Dnieper River. It was composed of steel and concrete, and stretched out one hundred meters tall. On one side, the water was as high as the dam. On the other, it was so shallow that it hardly covered the rocks. Imagine the higher water level as God's unconditional love that He wishes to pour into our lives. He has already paid for this love, and it is available to us. The magnitude of this love is included in salvation. In contrast, the lower water level represents what people actually have in their lives. Why is there such a big difference in these water levels? It is because of the dam. What would happen if the dam were pulled down? Tons of water would come crashing down and flood everything around the dam.

A similar type of dam is built into the hearts of people. It blocks the flow of God's love and doesn't allow it to work in our lives. Who built this dam? The Devil did, with the approval of the people. Who should tear this dam down? Humankind should, with the help of God. When a person tears down all the walls separating his or her heart from God, God's love fills that person's heart in a way that it has never been filled before.

The Source of Life

Life is very complicated. It generally includes the multifaceted aspects of marriage, family, interpersonal relationships, health, finances, business, service obligations, vocational responsibilities, and many more. Most people expend great effort trying to establish order in these areas, yet they always seem to come up short. Sometimes, after repeated efforts to establish order, the person gives up, deciding that success is beyond his grasp. Unfortunately, few understand that the source of each person's problems is not found superficially, but rather internally. The Bible says that the wellspring of all areas of a person's life is in his or her heart. "Keep your heart with all diligence, for out of it spring the issues of life" (Prov. 4:23).

If a person has poor thoughts, he or she will always be beggar. If a person thinks as a slave, he or she will always be slave, and so on.

Allow me to present another example. Imagine that many years ago, on a high mountaintop there was a spring with crystal clear water. As it flowed downhill, it turned into a stream, then a river, and then a great sea. The river and the sea were once full of life, but then something unfortunate occurred. On top of this mountain, right at the spring, a businessman built a factory that made chemicals. He emptied the pipes that discharged waste right into that spring. The waste poisoned the river and sea, and everything in them began to die. People noticed this and began to build a cleaning tower in an attempt to clean the sea. Though they put great effort cleaning the seawater, it did not improve. These people then met others who called their sea cleaning efforts useless, and they started to clean the river instead. However, the river cleaning efforts didn't result in an improvement of the water quality either. Finally, a few brave souls decided to climb up the mountain. When they reached the spring, they discovered the pipes were the source of the deadly toxins. The factory was immediately destroyed, the pipes were removed, and clean water once again rejuvenated the river and sea.

Before one can guard his or her heart, each person must first understand both the contents of his or her heart and how it has been burdened by living on this sinful earth. There is a philosophical question: "Does existence determine conscience, or does conscience determine existence?" It is found to be true that as long as each person is being formed as an individual, then his or her existence (surroundings, upbringing, relationships, culture, school, environment, religion, and different experiences) forms the specific thoughts, habits, and character with which that person will live until death. These aspects of a person's mentality will, in turn, influence all areas of his or her life.

If a person grew up in a good environment, was raised properly, dearly loved, had friendly relationships, saw good examples and experienced the kindness of others, then he would have a proper mentality that predestined him to a healthy way of life. But if a person experienced serious emotional trauma, taunting, beating, violence, betrayal, and other negative influences, or if he grew up without a father or mother, didn't receive adequate love, or experienced rejection, then without God's intervention, he would never live a normal life. He would be unable to have a close and deep relationship with God, and he would see everything and everyone through the prism of his wounds and pain. His notion of God and God's love would always be distorted.

Suppose there were three skinny woven trees planted in one pot. If these trees grew together in this same pot for twenty years, it would be impossible to untwist them because they would have become one whole tree. A person's life is like this tree. As the person grows and develops, he or she can become so entwined by his or her sicknesses, fears, and assorted vices that they become a part of the person's existence, forming his or her character, way of thinking, and entire being. Only the Holy Spirit, through the Word of God, is able to deliver an individual from all the negative things he or she has been conditioned by.

Masks

Humankind was created in the likeness and image of God. He was complete and did not know sin. The first humans, Adam and Eve, had a close relationship with God and with each other. They were both naked and unashamed because God's glory covered their nakedness, and as a result, they felt comfortable in front of each other and in the presence of God. They had nothing to hide. But then the most awful tragedy occurred. Being deceived by the Devil, they both sinned before God. In consequence, God's glory disappeared, and they found themselves to be naked. To cover themselves up, they made themselves coverings from leaves, and when God came to meet with them, being moved by fear and feelings of guilt, Adam and Eve tried to hide from Him.

Every person is an expert at covering up his or her sins. Humankind learns this trick from the Devil, who pushes us into sin. When a sin is committed, the Devil advises us to hide it so that no one will see or know about it. Unfortunately, the Devil has taught this not only to unbelievers, but to Christians as well. By hiding their sins, people clothe themselves in masks. A person comes to church, and the pastor asks, "How are you doing?" The person puts on a fake smile and answers, "Praise God, all is good." The person comes home, and his or her spouse or parents ask, "Where have you been?" The person is afraid to answer honestly, and so he or she says, "I got held up with my friends." A husband and wife have a disagreement discussing their relationship in their bedroom in raised voices. They come out with reddened faces and plastic smiles, assuring their children that "everything is fine." In this way, people's lives have been turned into an utter masquerade. It is impossible to be open with God when you are hiding from people.

Each masked individual is found to be a hypocrite, a condition that God absolutely hates. We don't only hide our sin under our masks. Under our masks we hide our bitterness, pain, fears, rejection, and many other things. A person in a mask will be unable to build healthy relationships with other people, and most importantly, with God. When the masks come off, everyone discovers what is underneath. Only when all the matters are brought to light can they finally be dealt with and resolved. This is why the apostle Paul taught Timothy this: "Take heed to yourself and to the doctrine. Continue in them: for in doing this you will both save yourself and those who hear you" (1 Tim. 4:16).

Under the word doctrine, the apostle Paul refers to God's Word.

God's Word completes a multitude of different functions. One of the roles it plays is as a spiritual mirror of the soul. Mirrors don't change us; they only give us the opportunity to see our true, unedited conditions. In the light of God's Word, each person should constantly run a self-analysis because through this, the Holy Spirit can show each person the areas and moments in his or her life that desperately need order and change.

The very first thing that the Holy Spirit shows us through the Word is sin.

CHAPTER 3

Sin

S in is the first piece of the dam that separates humankind from God. Sin robs people of God's blessings and prevents them from experiencing His fatherly love. "Behold, the Lord's hand is not shortened, that it cannot save; nor his ear heavy, that it cannot hear. But your iniquities have you from your God; and your sins have hid His face from you, so that He will not hear" (Isa. 59:1–2).

Sin separates humankind from God, filling people's hearts with fear and feelings of guilt. Sin is from the Devil, and it represents lawlessness and rebellion against God. "Whoever commits sin also commits lawlessness: for sin lawlessness. He who sins is of the devil, for he has sinned from the beginning. For this purpose the Son of God was manifested, that He might destroy the works of the devil" (1 John 3:4, 8).

Sin defiles people, poisons their lives, destroys their relationships, brings sickness and bondage, brings rise to curse, and leads to demonic strongholds. Sinful acts always produce death. Many unbelieving people do not bother to hide their sins. Christians, enlightened by God's truth, understand that sin is evil and that it is shameful. However, in spite of this, some Christians allow sin to live in their hearts and rule over them. By this, they separate themselves from God's love. This does not mean that God stops loving them; they have simply covered themselves, and God's love is unable to penetrate this wall.

There are Christians who live for years with the sense of guilt for sins committed in the past. Although they have repented, they don't have enough faith to receive God's forgiveness. They do not have confidence in God, and their conscience torments them. Because of this, they do not raise their hands to God; they can't enter into their calling, and as a result they are unable to fulfill the will of God. Their prayers go unanswered, not because God doesn't wish to answer them, but because these Christians don't have the faith to receive anything from God.

> For if our heart condemns us, God is greater than our heart, and knows all things. Beloved, if our heart does not condemn us, we have confidence toward God. And whatever we ask we receive from Him, because we keep His commandments and do those things that are pleasing in His sight. (1 John 3:20–22)

There are other people who continually sin in a certain area. They sin and repent, then sin and repent again, and are unable to break free of this pattern. Their conscience also torments them, and they feel weak and defeated. They experience the same sense of failure as the first group. Although they may have moments of spiritual victory after specific instances of repentance, these moments don't last long, and once again they suffer defeat. A life of feeling such guilt leads to disappointment, despondency, and depression.

Finally, there is a third group of people that are consumed with sin, but they justify it and think that sin is a normal way of life. They have many arguments to defend their mind-set, which include the following:

- ❑ I love God.
- ❑ We are not under the law, but under grace.
- ❑ God looks at the heart.
- ❑ Everyone is doing it.
- ❑ God is good; He understands me.

But no matter how hard this third group tries to justify their sins, God and His Word remain unchanged.

The Ten Commandments

God established ten basic commandments that reveal His holiness and standards. In the New Testament, God's relationship toward sin does not change. As it was in the past, so it still stands today—God hates sin. God has always expected and will always expect His people to live holy lives. "But as He who called you is holy, you also be holy in all your conduct, because it is written, 'Be holy, for I am holy'" (1 Peter 1:15–16).

As in the time of both the Old and New Testaments, a sinful lifestyle is always followed by punishment (Heb. 12:6–11). There are Christians who maintain the idea that they are under grace and not under the law, and by this they try to justify their lawless lives. Grace, however, sets us free not only from the law but also from the power of sin (Rom. 6:14). This is why Christians who truly understand God's grace live a holy life, free from sin.

> But we know that the law is good if one uses lawfully, knowing this: that the law is not made for a righteous person, but for the lawless and insubordinate, for the ungodly and for sinners, for the unholy and profane, for murderers of fathers and murderers of mothers, for manslayers, for fornicators, for sodomites, for kidnappers, for liars, for perjurers, and if there is any other thing that is contrary to sound doctrine. (1 Tim. 1:8–10)

There are also so-called Christians who have never experienced true repentance, meaning that they have never experienced rebirth, or being born from above. They have never seen themselves perishing and judged and don't know what it means to be saved and justified.

The Ten Commandments are a form of guidance to bring us closer to Christ (Gal. 3:24). They reveal humankind's sinfulness.

First Commandment

I am the Lord your God, who brought you out of the land of Egypt, out of the house of bondage. You shall have no other gods before me. (Ex. 20:2–3)

Violation of this commandment involves worship of false gods, powers, and spirits, or anything except for the one and only Father God, Son, and Holy Spirit. It concerns those who participate in occult, practice witchcraft, fortune-telling, and calling up of spirits, or those who occupy themselves with listening to old wives' tales, studying the horoscope, believing in superstition, and all others things that are connected with occult practices. If there is something in the life of a person that causes him or her to sacrifice his or her relationship with God, then that person is breaking the very first commandment. Breaking the first commandment always leads to the violation of the rest of the commandments.

Second Commandment

You shall not make for yourself a carved image—any likeness of anything that is in heaven above, or that is in the earth beneath, or that is in the water under the earth; you shall not bow down to them nor serve them. For I, the Lord your God, am a jealous God, visiting the iniquity of the fathers upon the children to the third and fourth generation of those who hate Me, but showing mercy to thousands, to those who love Me and keep My commandments. (Ex. 20:4–6)

Violation of this commandment involves the worship of charms, images, and statues in the form of people, animals, fish, or other objects. It also involves deification and prayers to various objects, the wearing of charms, shark's teeth, and good luck bracelets, and using horseshoes and different objects to supernaturally bring health, success, well-being, and protection. All forms of idolatry are in violation of this commandment.

Third Commandment

You shall not take the name of the Lord your God in vain, for the Lord will not hold him guiltless who takes His name in vain. (Ex. 20:7)

This commandment forbids pronouncing the name of God without respect. It is a warning against using God's name for the purpose of connecting words in lies, curses, and dirty jokes.

Fourth Commandment

Remember the Sabbath day, to keep it holy. Six days you shall labor an do all your word, but the seventh day is the Sabbath of the Lord your God. In it you shall do no work: you, nor your son, nor your daughter, nor your male servant, nor your female servant, nor your cattle, nor your stranger who is within your gates. For in six days the Lord made the heavens and the earth, the sea, and all that is in them, and rested the seventh day. Therefore the Lord blessed the Sabbath day and hallowed it. (Ex. 20:8–11)

God commanded us to work six days. Laziness and parasitism, life at the expense of others, and also, in contrast, an overbusy and hectic life leading to a lack of time to serve and worship God, are found to be an obstruction of this commandment. In the area of finances, God commanded each person to give back a tenth of his or her earnings, and in the form of time, God asked for a seventh. One of every seven days should be dedicated to the Lord. On this day, one leaves all of life's vanity, and all his or her attention becomes focused on God and community.

Fifth Commandment

> Honor your father and mother, that your days may be long upon the land which the Lord your God is giving you. (Ex. 20:12)

This commandment is a warning against disobedience, scorn, evil speaking toward parents, and pronounced rebellion against authority.

Sixth Commandment

> You shall not murder. (Ex. 20:13)

This commandment is a warning against murder, abortion of any form, calling someone a fool, and hatred toward a brother or sister.

Seventh Commandment

> You shall not commit adultery. (Ex. 20:14)

This commandment is a warning against adultery, fornication, lust, and all forms of sexual sin and sexual indiscretion.

Eighth Commandment

> You shall not steal. (Ex. 20:15)

This commandment is a warning against stealing, not paying wages, deception in paying taxes, not tithing, and not paying off a debt on time.

Ninth Commandment

> You shall not bear false witness against your neighbor. (Ex. 20:16)

This commandment is a warning against false witness, gossip, slander, rumors, and passing on unverified information. This also includes the use of truthful information if it is done with the intention of discrediting a person.

Tenth Commandment

> You shall not covet your neighbor's house; you shall not covet you neighbor's wife, nor his male servant nor his female servant, nor his ox, nor his donkey, or anything that is your neighbor's. (Ex. 20:17)

This commandment is a warning against desiring the possessions of those around you, which is also known as envy.

Very often, the breaking of one commandment automatically leads to the breaking of other commandments. It's impossible to break the seventh commandment, for example, without also breaking the eighth and tenth. A man who commits adultery had first desired another woman, and then he stole her from her real or future husband. Violation of any commandment is always automatically tied with the violation of the first commandment, because the violator is deliberately ignoring God's decree and putting other matters' priority before Him.

The Bible says that the wages of sin is death (Rom. 6:23). On the basis of God's law, the whole world is guilty before God because all have sinned and are deprived of the glory of God. That's why the Bible says that there is no one righteous, not a single one (Rom. 3:10, 23).

God created humankind to rule over the earth and to live a free life. By yielding to the temptation of Satan, humankind fell away from God. The second that humankind disobeyed God, sin infiltrated the hearts of the people and made them its slave. In the heart of humankind grew something supernatural and foreign to them. Just like cancer cells, sin metastasized and spread throughout all of humankind. Sin is the nature of the Devil and stands in opposition with God.

Sin is stronger than human nature, and this is why each person that sins is a slave to it. Sin lives in absolutely all people and gets passed through genetic lineages from ancestors to their descendents. The Bible says that everyone has sinned and has been stripped of the glory of God. There is no righteous person on this earth.

Sin has many different desires that are unnatural to people. God calls these sinful desires lusts. Lusts have blended in so much with our natural and normal desires that we accept these sinful desires like our own. So when a person develops sinful desires, it seems to the person that it is he or she who desires these things, when in fact it is the desires of his or her sinful nature living within that are driving that person.

Why are there so many restrictions and boundaries in this day and age? From a young age, each child hears, "Don't touch, don't go, don't watch, don't drink, don't smoke, don't lie, don't fight, you can't." And with this "no," there is usually no rhyme or reason. At home, everything is forbidden and has boundaries. School has its own rules too, as do roads, companies, and governments. Wherever you turn, something is forbidden.

When children are small, it seems to them that when they grow up, they will be allowed to do everything. But as these children grow, they find that the restrictions and boundaries are no fewer, but the punishment of their violation becomes a bit more serious.

Each person as an individual, and the community as a whole, tries to tame and restrict this "animal" inside each person called sin. And if each person doesn't wish to fight this animal and gives it freedom, then this person, along with the animal, hides behinds bars.

If the spiritual world opened up before us today, and we were able to see into the souls of people bound by the chains of sin, we would be horrified by what we saw. Today, the word sin is unpopular. We usually switch the term out for something less offensive, like bad habits, addictions, human weaknesses, and so on.

God hates sin because it destroys a person, deprives a person of human dignity, restricts a person, and leads a person to eternal damnation. God created each person uniquely by giving him or her gifts, individual talents, and abilities, but sin destroys all this. Just as a virus infiltrating a computer destroys all the programs and slows its function, sin is able to paralyze any area of a person's life.

Sin deprives mothers and fathers of parental feelings, and they become harsh toward their children. Sin sows discord between friends. Because of sinful habits, people lose their jobs, health, and family happiness; families are destroyed, children become orphans, people fall into bondage and a lifestyle of murder, rape and war. At the hands of sin, so many talents are buried, many premature deaths occur, and automobile catastrophes and tragedies increase.

All human efforts, methods, and determination are useless against sin. On this earth, there is no such medicine or strength that could rid this terminally ill humanity of its "leprosy." People think that if they satisfy their sinful desires, then they will find relief, but the more they satisfy their lusts, the more of an appetite they acquire, and the more they begin to fester. The leash on which sin holds its victims with each time gets shorter and shorter.

I once heard about how wolves get killed. When the woods become too populated with wolves, people come together to form a hunt. The clever part about the plan is that these wolves bring their own destruction. In the winter, the hunters take double-edged knives and dip them into animal blood. When the blood dries, they're doused with water and put out into the cold so the water can freeze. After that, the hunters bury these icy knives in the forest so that only the tips stick out and leave.

The wolves, sensing the smell of blood, gather in the forest and start to lick the blades of the knives. Cutting their tongues, they don't notice that they are licking their own blood. Their hunger gets so strong that they cannot tear themselves from the weapons, and this is how they perish.

In this same fashion, the Devil fools human souls, leaving them stuck in their lies, envy, anger, hate, alcohol, drugs, and other vices.

Sin is the main cause of humankind's problems. Sin separates us from God, brings sickness, destroys relationships and marriages, and brings curse, demonic addictions, and death to the life of man. The only means of destroying sin is through the blood of Jesus Christ.

> But now, once at the end of the ages, He has appeared to put away sin by the sacrifice of Himself. (Heb. 9:26)

> And the blood of Jesus, His Son, cleanses us from all sin. (1 John 1:7)

CHAPTER 4

Moral Purity

One of the greatest gifts that God gave humankind is sexuality. Sexual attraction is not dirty or sinful, but pure and holy. In making man and woman, God said, "Be fruitful multiply; fill the earth ..." (Gen. 1:28)

These were the very first words that God said to humankind, pronouncing the very first of His blessings. God blessed sexual relations between men and women. God limited this relationship to marriage, and only in marriage does He bless it. However, to great misfortune, the Enemy has caused much evil to occur precisely in this area.

Sexuality in the Bible is often compared with water:

> Drink water from you own cistern, and running water from your own well. Should your fountains be dispersed abroad, streams of water in the streets? Let them be only your own, and not for strangers with you. Let your fountain be blessed, and rejoice with the wife of your youth. As a loving doe and a graceful deer ... (Prov. 5:15–19)

A garden enclosed is my sister, my spouse, a spring shut up, a fountain sealed ... A fountain of gardens, a well of living waters, and streams from Lebanon. (Song 4:12, 15)

Before marriage, a woman should be like a sealed well and spring. The first one who should drink from that spring is her beloved, the one with whom she has made a covenant. This comes after she is united in lawful marriage, and this is how God created woman. At the time of the first encounter there is an unsealing, through which appears blood. This represents a blood covenant that is made between men and women.

The goal of the Devil is to pull people into sexual relationships both before marriage or outside of marriage and therefore rob them of healthy sexual relations in marriage. This is why the apostle Paul taught, "For this is the will of God your sanctification: that you should abstain from sexual immorality; that each of you should know how to possess his own vessel in sanctification and honor, not in passion of lust, like the Gentiles who do not know God ..." (1 Thess. 4:3–5).

Today we live in a corrupt world that promotes depraved lifestyles. For some people, sex is like a sport. Sexual relationships before marriage and outside of marriage fill people's lives with problems, sickness, destruction, bondage, and demonic possession. The Bible says that God judges fornicators and adulterers (Heb. 13:4).

Ocean water is a beneficial blessing to people. But when it goes beyond its shores and a tsunami is formed, that same water turns into a curse that brings great injury and destruction. This is exactly how it works with sex. In marriage, it is a blessing, and it brings life, unity, joy, pleasure, and satisfaction. But when it is performed outside of marriage, it brings bitterness, tears, broken relationships, ruined families, ruined health and finances, and the loss of the presence and anointing of God.

> Flee sexual immorality. Every sin that a man does is outside the body, but he who commits sexual immorality sins against his own body. (1 Cor. 6:18)

Most often sexual problems begin in childhood or at the moment of a person's sexual maturity. A ten-year-old child may commit a sin that is usually only associated with adults, which can happen even if no one taught that child how to do this. Such type of sin signifies an inherited curse that came to the child from his or her parents or grandparents.

Other children are taught how to sin by someone else, or they are exposed to sin and pulled into it. A third category of children start an early sexual life because of rejection, spiritual wounds, offenses, unforgiveness, or a lack of love in their parents' home. Perhaps an individual was raped, and through such an experience, they inherited a spirit of adultery and lust.

There are many reasons for sexual sin, but the outcome is always the same—the person falls into trouble. There are so many types of sexual sin that a normal person wouldn't even imagine of. To great misfortune, however, these sins are seen among believers as well as unbelievers. People bring sinful baggage into their Christian lives, are ashamed to confess their lack of strength to fight these sins, and they don't know how to escape them. That's why such people choose to live behind a mask of piety, remaining defiled in their minds and consciences.

Sexual impurity is: adultery, fornication, exhibiting a naked body, prostitution, pornography, masturbation, sexual perversion, sex with relatives, sex with people of the same gender, sex with animals, sex with children, sex with demons or evil spirits, lust, peeping, and rape.

The Bible says that to be united with a woman is to become one flesh with her.

> Or do you not know that he who is joined to a harlot is one body with her? For 'the two,' He says, 'shall become one flesh.' (1 Cor. 6:16)

Through playing the field and adulterous relationships, improper spiritual bonds are formed. If a man has had several partners, then he is divided inside. It is very hard for him to love his wife with all his heart, as part of his soul is left with the others with whom he has had intimate relations. If one of those partners has been involved in witchcraft or occultism, then this man may inherit that partner's curses and demonic possession.

Jesus came to destroy all the works of the Devil and to set all people free. Today He continues to heal broken destinies, return lost honor, and restore people completely to their places as a valuable individuals.

> He who covers his sins will not prosper, but whoever confesses and forsakes them will have mercy. (Prov. 28:13)

God has no desire to put individuals in a corner. He loves each person and doesn't want anyone to die. He waits for individuals to turn from their evil deeds, and that is when He shows His mercy, which is always above judgment.

CHAPTER 5

Revelation of the Sacrifice of Jesus Christ

And as Moses lifted up the serpent in the wilderness, even so must the Son of Man be lifted up, that whoever believes in Him should not perish but have eternal life. For God so loved the world that He gave His only begotten Son, that whoever believes in Him should not perish but have everlasting life. (John 3:14–16)

When the people of Israel complained in the desert, poisonous snakes attacked them. The venom from these snakes was deadly, and many people died. The people began to cry out to God, and God told Moses to make a brass serpent and hold it up as a sign before the face of the people. By gazing at the serpent, the affected people escaped death.

This event symbolizes the sacrifice of Jesus Christ. Just as a single glance at the brass serpent destroyed the power of the snake's poisonous venom, faith in the crucified Jesus destroys the power of sin and death and saves humankind from eternal punishment. The only Savior from sin and all its consequences is the crucified and risen Jesus Christ. Jesus tasted death for all of humankind on the shameful cross. The cross of Calvary, on which the Son of God was crucified, is the center of the gospel and our salvation. "For the message of the cross is foolishness to those who are perishing, but to us who are being saved it is the power of God" (1 Cor. 1:18).

The cross of Jesus is a great wealth to all those who are saved. The apostle Paul, despite all that he had and possessed, wanted only to glory in the cross of God. Through this cross he was crucified to the world, and the world was crucified to Him (Gal. 6:14). The cross, or what happened on the cross, reveals all the horrors of humankind's sin, the incorruptibility of God's judgment, the greatness of God's holiness, and the limitless love of God for people.

The cross was the purpose of Jesus Christ's life. For its sake, He was born, for it He prepared thirty-three and a half years, and on it He finished His earthly life. If Christ had been born, taught, healed the sick, cast out demons, and done many more good things but didn't go to the cross, then we would not have been saved. We all would still have perished forever.

But he was wounded for our transgressions, he was bruised for our iniquities; the chastisement for our peace was upon Him, and by his stripes we are healed. We all like sheep have gone astray; we have turned, every one, to his own way; and the Lord has laid on him the iniquity of us all ... Yet it pleased the Lord to bruise Him; He has put Him to grief ... (Isa. 53:5–6, 10)

Not long ago, a film called The Passion of the Christ was released and was created by Mel Gibson. The actor who played the role of Jesus Christ was supposed to play his part as written by the director. All his words, movements, and actions needed to go along with the scenes, and it was necessary for this actor to show all the horrors of the suffering of Jesus Christ.

It is indeed impossible to watch this film indifferently. The film displays a tremendous amount of blood, violence, and taunting. Yet this is just a film in which actors played. What Christ experienced was reality.

Even before He was born onto this earth, Jesus's life also had a written script. The loving heavenly Father had written this terrible script for His only beloved Son. In this script, Jesus would be born, live, and die. Through the hands of the prophets of the Old Testament, Father God described in detail all that His Son would need to go through and accomplish. Jesus knew perfectly the cup from which He would have to drink. In this cup were found all the sins of men who had lived on the earth from Adam up to the very last sinner. He took upon Himself all sickness, curse, shame, embarrassment, rejection, betrayal, and all of the evil of humankind. It was necessary for Jesus to experience all the things that people experience because through this sacrifice, He could understand suffering and the needs of each person and acquire the ability to help.

Jesus experienced betrayal in order to understand and help those who have been betrayed. He was abandoned by all when He especially needed them, so that He could be near the lonely. He was slandered and judged unfairly. He was beaten in the face, His beard was torn out, and He was spit at. He experienced rejection when they gave preference to the criminal and murderer Barabbas, and the Roman soldiers whipped Him. Jesus endured thirty-nine lashes, the whip ripping flesh from His back with its sharp spikes and laid bare His insides. Thirty-nine lashes—thirty-nine kinds of sicknesses. Jesus practically and realistically took upon His body all the sickness and weakness of the world so that by His wounds all believers would receive healing.

On Jesus's head was laid a crown of thorns—a symbol of the curse (Gen. 3:17–18). Upon Himself He took all the curses deserved by people, and hanging on the cursed cross, made Himself cursed for all so that all the blessings of God would come upon all believers. "Christ has redeemed us from the curse of the law, having become a curse for us (for it is written, 'Cursed is everyone who hangs on a tree.'" (Gal. 3:13)

Jesus's clean hands were pierced with rusty nails so that the hands of God's children would be made clean, successful, and pleasing for every work of God. His feet were beaten so that the feet of His followers could take the message of His kingdom to the ends of the earth. He thirsted so that we would be able to drink and hungered so that we would be made full. He was put to shame before the crowd to take away our shame and clothe us in glory. He was rejected by heaven and earth so that we would be forever accepted into His family. He tasted death for all so that all who believe in Him would not perish, but would have life and life abundantly. Jesus spilled His precious blood so that we would be forgiven, redeemed, and justified.

In the crucified Christ are hidden all the riches of humankind. All that a person's spirit, soul, and body need are hidden in His sacrifice. No matter how much we read about the sacrifice of Christ and of His torment and suffering on the cross, on our own, we will never understand all that was accomplished on the cross. Only the Holy Spirit can reveal this. The Holy Spirit not only reveals this, but He also longs to make all the treasures of the sacrifice of the Lamb of God the genuine possession of each Christian.

On the cross Jesus shattered the power of sin. Through His unblemished sacrifice, He reconciled heaven and earth. Jesus's sacrifice satisfied God's principle of justice and completed the full work of salvation. This is why, while hanging on the cross, Jesus looked back and saw the perfection of God's work and proclaimed, "It is finished!"

Jesus fulfilled all that had been written about Him. Today Jesus is the intercessor and high priest before His Father. Today He represents all who humbly receive all the riches of His precious sacrifice. With His shed blood Jesus went into the very heavens and obtained eternal redemption for us.

Allow me to give an example through a story: Once there lived two close friends in a small village. From childhood, they attended the same schools, sat behind the same desk, and spent all their free time together. They lived as blood brothers.

After graduation, one of them, along with his parents, moved to a bigger city. Upon finishing college, he went on to become a lawyer and eventually a judge. The other one, having stayed put, connected with a bad crowd and became a thief.

Many years passed, and the thief was caught and brought to court. In the courtroom, the two old friends reunited after many years: one occupied the place of a judge, and the other was the one being judged. They recognized each other right away. The convicted man hoped that his friend would help him, but the judge did not give any indication that they knew each other. Being an honest man, and not wanting to break the law, he gave his friend a just verdict. The convicted thief was obligated to pay an outrageous fine, or he would be put behind bars for a long time.

Immensely discouraged with his friend, the thief sat in his cell with his head in his hands. Bitterness and hopelessness filled his heart. During this time, the judge stood up from his chair, went into his office, and took off his robe. He took out his checkbook and wrote out a check for the full amount of the fine. He approached his old friend, softly touched his shoulder, and holding out his check, said, "I have not forgotten about our friendship. If you want, you may pay with my money." This judge was in no way obligated to pay because, in essence, he wasn't the guilty one.

We have all violated the law of God and deserve eternal punishment in hell. But God, loving us, gave His only Son, Jesus Christ, for death. Through His death and resurrection, God now justifies every sinner when he turns to Him with repentance.

Repentance

"He who covers his sins will not prosper, but whoever confesses and forsakes them will have mercy" (Prov. 28:13). An individual who lives in sin cannot be successful. Sin is the first obstacle that needs to be removed from a person's life. When a person sincerely repents, the blood of Christ abolishes sin.

Why didn't the Sadducees and Pharisees receive Christ? When John the Baptist came, he preached about repentance. The Sadducees and Pharisees knew that they needed to repent, but it was their pride that prevented them from doing this, so one day, Jesus told the Pharisees, who had brought before Him a woman caught in the act of adultery, that the one among them who was without sin should cast the first stone. After judging their own consciences, the Sadducees and Pharisees all left, for they understood that they had all sinned. When John the Baptist called them to confess their sins, they knew perfectly well what he was asking them to do, but because of their pride, they couldn't do it.

By their actions, or better to say their inaction, the Sadducees and Pharisees consciously hardened their hearts. Therefore, when Jesus came, the one who was indeed the truth, they took stones into their hands to kill Him. In spite of all the miracles that He performed and the irrefutable facts and proofs they saw, the Sadducees and Pharisees did not want to accept Jesus. Acceptance was already beyond their ability.

The concept of repentance is described very clearly in the parable of the prodigal son. Having offended, humiliated, and shamed his father, the youngest son left his father's house to pursue the attractions of a free, sinful lifestyle. As he left, the son had no idea of the future consequences of this decision.

When the Devil offers and advertises sin, he never talks about its consequences. Someone once said that sin has three specialties:

1. It always takes a person further than he or she wants to go (entices).
2. It always holds a person longer than he or she wants to be held (enslaves).
3. It always costs a person more than he or she had planned to pay (robs).

When the money that the father had given the son ran out, all of the son's friends suddenly left him. Unemployment ensued, and the son's hunger led him to a pigsty. The pigs had better conditions than he did, but the son's new master didn't even let him eat what the pigs ate. Only then did the son start to think, What was life like before this? He was living in an illusion, but his hungry stomach finally led him to his senses. Some people need this kind of therapy. Finding himself without his father's love, money, family, work, education, decent clothes, warmth, or comfort, the son's momentary happiness burst like a bubble.

In that moment of despair, the son remembered his kind father and his father's house. Only then did the son begin to understand what he had really done. He saw before his eyes the gentle, crying face of his father and the way he looked the last time he had seen him. The son had been ashamed, bitter, and offended, and after examining his crime, he realized he had been wrong. "I will arise and go to my father, and will say to him, 'Father, I have sinned against heaven and before you, and I am no longer worthy

to be called your son. Make me like one of your hired servants'" (Luke 15:18–19).

The son made his decision and then got up and left for
home.

During all those years of separation, the father had continued to love his son. He fully knew where the road his
son had chosen would lead. When the father saw the son's
familiar silhouette from afar and the dear features similar
to his own, he knew for sure that his son was approaching.
The father ran out to meet his son, fell on his neck, and
hugged and kissed him.

This story illustrates how the loving heavenly Father
waits for and receives all those prodigal sons who have
been lured away by sin. The Father knows the end result
of that kind of lifestyle. Two thousand years ago, the Father God laid all of our sins upon His Son, Jesus. John the
Baptist pointed to Him and said, "Behold! The Lamb of
God who takes away the sin of the world!" (John 1:29)

In the Old Testament, if an individual sinned, he or
she took an animal to the priest, laid hands on it, and
confessed the sin. Through the laying on of hands and
confession, the sin was transferred from the person to
the animal. Sin is spiritual and impossible to kill, and
for that reason the animal became the carrier of the sin.
Through the death of the animal, the person's sin was
also destroyed.

The blood of animals was actually an inadequate way
to destroy sin, and that is why it was necessary for Jesus

to come down from heaven, take on the body of a man, live an absolutely holy life, take upon Himself the sins of the whole world, and finally go to the cross to destroy sin forever. That is what He did for us. Praise be to God!

In order to be set free from sin today, we must lay our sins upon Jesus through confession and sincere repentance. Jesus no longer dies for our sins; He already did that once and forever. The only thing necessary now is for humankind to do its part.

There are many people who sincerely regret the sins that they have committed. They cry and condemn themselves, and they even confess their sins to others. However, even if they do these things, they are not forgiven. Judas, who betrayed Jesus, did these things too, but it didn't help him. Regret is only a part of what true repentance means.

The most important part of repentance is a change in one's mentality, leading to a change in lifestyle. To repent means to turn from sin and to go in the opposite direction. The prodigal son judged Himself, and perhaps He even cried. However, His repentance was not complete until He left His old way of life and went back to His Father.

There are three types of judgment:

1. God's judgment at the white throne
2. God's judgment of His children while they are on the earth
3. A person's judgment of him- or herself

God always offers people the right to judge their own sins on the basis of His Word. If a person judges him- or herself by bringing his or her sins into the light, repents, and turns from them, God forgives and redeems that person (1 Cor. 11:31–32). If a person doesn't want to let go of his or her sins, then God in His great love punishes that person, prompting him or her to true repentance. In this way, God judges the individual on earth so that he or she will not be judged with the world. If a person is stubborn and dies before repenting of his or her sins, then God will judge that person at the white throne.

Most importantly, repentance involves an individual's heart. A person comprehends what he or she has done, repents of his or her sin, regrets it, and then by the decision of his or her will, turns from his or her old way of living and seeks God. The person walks into the embrace of His loving Father, who is waiting to receive him or her.

Repentance is a display of humility (James 4:5–10). To repent means to obey God. To live in sin means to live in rebellion toward God; it is a sign of humankind's pride, which is hateful and offensive to God.

God always forgives those who repent, and He does so instantly. He accepts them into His loving arms, washes them, and restores their rights as heirs. This is followed by a celebration, brought together by God the Father Himself.

Prayer of Repentance

Dear heavenly Father! I come to You in the name of Your Son, Jesus Christ. I ask You to forgive me of my sins (confess your sins, saying them by name). I repent before You and renounce all of my sins. Wash me with Your holy blood, cleanse my heart, and live in it. I believe that Jesus died for my sins and rose for my redemption. I confess Jesus Christ to be my Lord and Savior. I thank You that right now, You are forgiving me of all my sins. I accept Your love and Your forgiveness. Glory to You, Lord! Amen.

CHAPTER 6

Bitterness

T he other most common reason behind heartache that serves as a huge obstacle for accepting God's love is bitterness and unforgiveness. In the New Testament, Jesus repeatedly spoke of the need to forgive offenders and to have right relationships with people. Jesus taught about the laws and principals of forgiveness that work in God's kingdom.

> Therefore the kingdom of heaven is like a certain king who wanted to settle accounts with his servants. And when he had begun to settle accounts, one was brought to him who owed him ten thousand talents. But as he was not able to pay, his master commanded that he be sold, with his wife and children and all that he had, and that payment be made. The servant therefore fell down before him, saying, "Master, have patience with me, and I will pay you all." Then the master of that servant was moved

with compassion, released him, and forgave him the debt.

But that servant went out and found one of his fellow servants who owed him a hundred denarii; and he laid hands on him and took him by the throat, saying, "Pay me what you owe!" So his fellow servant fell down at his feet and begged him, saying, "Have patience with me, and I will pay you all." And he would not, but went and threw him into prison till he should pay the debt. So when his fellow servants saw what had been done, they were very grieved, and came and told their master all that had been done. Then his master, after he had called him, said to him, "You wicked servant! I forgave you all that debt because you begged me. Should you not also have had compassion on your fellow servant, just as I had pity on you?" And his master was angry, and delivered him to the torturers until he should pay all that was due to him.

So My heavenly Father also will do to you if each of you, from his heart, does not forgive his brother his trespasses. (Matt. 18:23–35)

Jesus calls sin a debt. The slave described in the verses above was so guilty before his master that he could never pay for his sin and crime, but the master, being merciful, forgave him all of his debt. The slave, however, did not want to forgive a friend who had once offended him. He sent him to prison unforgiven and waited for what he was owed. When the master found out about this, he was angry. Who was he angry with? He was angry with the one who was offended and unwilling to forgive. He demanded that the evil servant pay the debt that he had previously forgiven. Jesus said that the heavenly Father would do the same to each one of those who does not forgive his brother for his sins.

In the Sermon on the Mount, Jesus taught us how to pray. The prayer includes this phrase: "And forgive us our debts, as we forgive our debtors" (Matt. 6:12).

Then Jesus said: "For if you forgive men their trespasses, your heavenly Father will also forgive you. But if you do not forgive men their trespasses, neither will your Father forgive your trespasses" (Matt. 6:14–15).

Our relationship with our heavenly Father is directly connected to how we forgive those who offend us. If a person does not forgive those who have offended him or her, then that person cannot depend on God's mercy and falls under God's anger. Through unforgiveness, people open the doors of their lives to the Devil. "Be angry, and do not sin": do not let the sun go down on your wrath, and nor give place to the devil" (Eph. 4:26–27).

Offense and unforgiveness destroy a person's relationship with his or her loved ones and with God. God removes His protection, and the individual falls into the hands of the tormentor. The tormentor is the power of darkness, sickness, depression, worry, ulcers, heart disease, insomnia, arthritis, and much more. Sometimes people carry bitterness in their hearts for years and even decades. There are even Christians who boast about their offenses as if they were medals, saying, "Look how I was offended!"

Of course, if a person is wounded, beaten, ridiculed, raped, denigrated, betrayed, mugged, or robbed, he or she is truly a victim of crime, and such crimes are worthy of punishment. But God in His Word forbids taking revenge for oneself or carrying offense, bitterness, and hatred in one's heart. He commands us to give the offending person to Him for judgment and vengeance. "Beloved, do not avenge yourselves, but rather give place to wrath; for it is written: 'Vengeance is Mine, I will repay,' says the Lord" (Rom. 12:19).

God has forgiven us all so much that we could never pay Him back. We all deserve eternal punishment, but in His great love and mercy, the heavenly Father forgave us all. Our forgiveness cost Him very much. When the master in Matthew 19 forgave the servant, he lost ten thousand talents from his treasury. When God forgave us, it cost His beloved Son, Jesus Christ, the torment of Calvary.

Very often people seek and demand fairness for themselves. They take a firm stand on the position of justice, thinking that they have the full right to be offended; after all, someone has treated them unfairly. As long as people live on earth, God almost never treats them justly. God's

67

mercy is above justice, and God teaches His children to live in this same way. Forgiveness is undeserved mercy. God shows us this underserved mercy, and He expects us to show it to others as well. "For judgment is without mercy to the one who has shown no mercy. Mercy triumphs over judgment" (James 2:13).

Therefore, the person who does not want to forgive brings judgment upon him- or herself.

The words of the New Testament are intended directly for the person who reads them. If an individual is offended, then he or she is obligated first of all to forgive the offender. Secondly, the person must go and talk with his or her offender in order to lead the offender to repentance and restore his or her relationship with the offender (Matt. 18:15–18). Conversely, if a person knows that he or she has offended someone else, then he or she is obligated to ask for forgiveness from the victim and make peace with that person. Otherwise, the person will be thrown into prison (Matt. 5:23–26).

We see that both the offender and the offended can be thrown into prison. The only way to escape the prison of conflict is to ask for forgiveness when guilty and to forgive others when you have been wronged. If this is not done, then the individual is thrown into prison, and his or her life is in the hands of the torturer.

Very often, offense is rooted in events that happened far back in childhood. Childhood and adolescence is a time when a person develops not only physiologically, but also emotionally and intellectually. It's a time when a person is most open, vulnerable, defenseless, and susceptible to both physical and physiological trauma. Taunting, unfair punishment, evil punishment, rejection, belittling, ridicule, violence, rape, betrayal, and assault always leave scars in the heart of a child. If a child is raised in a negative family environment, his or her growth is influenced, and his or her heart needs healing.

Most often, the wounds a person receives are from those whom he or she loves most, as well as from those who should love that person. Of Christ it is said, "And one will say to him, 'What are these wounds between your arms?' Then he will answer, 'Those with which I was wounded in the house of my friends'" (Zech. 13:6).

Many people suffer from wounds that they received during childhood in their parents' home, and very often these wounds lead to resentment toward their fathers and mothers. Such people often live their entire lives holding on to this resentment, and sometimes they die with it. For some, memories of a father or mother bring forth tears and heartache. They have certain moments in the past that they cannot forget and don't want to reminisce on them because they only find pain in these memories.

People can hold resentment toward others who are long dead, brothers and sisters, significant others and friends, neighbors and schoolteachers, husbands and wives, pastors, and very often, toward others Christians.

This resentment causes their hearts to bleed. Such people hide their wounds and pain, and sometimes their pride keeps them from acknowledging it even to themselves.

Many mistakes and bad decisions have been made as a result of offenses. A person may start to drink, smoke, use drugs, or cheat on his or her spouse. Some abandon their parents' home, church, God, or even their very lives, and the cause of all of this is unforgiveness. Resentment is very dangerous and destructive. Before a person can be set free from the vices that entered his or her life through offense, he or she must be set free from resentment itself. Unforgiveness is, in reality, an open door for sin and the Devil to come into one's life.

A young woman who was of marrying age was afraid to get married, and she didn't know why. When she was asked several questions, she tearfully answered that she had already forgiven all of her offenders, but the truth was that there were still deep wounds in her heart. If in remembering someone or some event from the past a person feels pain and wants to cry, that means that there is still pain and unforgiveness in that person's heart. When the girl truly forgave her offender and prayed for him, with a smile she said, "Now I want to get married."

Another situation involved a young man who began to drink after he found his wife in bed with his friend. He could not stop drinking until he forgave them both.

There was also a young man who couldn't speak to his father for more than ten minutes without getting annoyed. His pastor told him that he had a grudge against his father. Through tears, he answered that he had already forgiven him. The pastor told him that if he was crying, it meant that he had not fully forgiven. It turned out that his father was very strict with him during his childhood. After the man forgave his father and spoke to his father about this, their relationship was healed, and they became good friends.

Offense is like a knife plunged and left in the heart by the offender. The offender may not even suspect how much the one that he or she offended suffers. As long as the knife is in that person's heart, the offended one can never be healed. He or she can cry about it, tell everyone about it, and even ask God for healing, but no one and nothing can help the offended person until the knife is removed, and this can be done only by forgiveness.

Resentment makes a person evil, irritated, withdrawn, and aggressive. Any person who holds resentment may see and not like this conduct in him- or herself, but the person doesn't know how to change it. There is only one way out of this situation—to make the decision to forgive, ignore negative feelings, cease to seek or demand fairness, and say the words, "I forgive ..." To do so, the person must name the one who offended him or her and the things for which he or she forgives the offender. By this confession, a person turns from all bitterness, resentment, and unforgiveness and brings his or her wounded heart to Jesus, allowing Him to touch it. Only then does Jesus heal the person's wounds, blot out of his or her memory all the bitter memories, and fill his or her heart with His peace and love.

When an individual forgives, his or her heart is healed, and he or she can immediately receive physical healing, even without praying for it. This is because when the cause of many sicknesses is removed, it is easy to remove the symptoms. There was a man, for example, who had nerve damage along his thumb on his hand. The nerve began to get worse, and the pain began to spread to his shoulder, so the doctors predicted that he might die or become disabled. He experienced terrible pain, and he couldn't lift his arm or allow anyone to touch it. When he was prayed for and forgave, a miracle took place. He saw his arm lifted toward heaven and absolutely restored.

Prayer for the Forgiveness of Others

Dear heavenly Father! I ask You, in the name of Jesus Christ, to forgive me for carrying bitterness in my heart. I repent of this sin. You forgave me of all my sins, and right now, by Your Word, I wish to forgive all the people that have caused me pain. With all my heart, I forgive (list all the people that offended you and name specifically what it is that you are forgiving) my offenders. I love them, forgive them, and release them. I renounce all bitterness, resentment, and unforgiveness that I may have toward them. Jesus, I ask You to touch my wounded heart with Your pierced hand and heal all the wounds that were caused by people. Smooth from my mind all the bitter and painful memories. I accept Your love and healing right now. Thank You, Lord, that You healed my spiritual wounds. Amen.

Not Forgiving Yourself

Some people have a difficult time forgiving themselves. They may have once committed a crime or a sin, or perhaps they were negligent or avoided offering help to someone when they had the ability to do so. Maybe it was their fault that something irreparable happened—perhaps someone was even wounded or died. Maybe they have lived in sin for many years and it caused their marriage to fall apart, or their children to walk away from God, and today, many years later, they can't forgive themselves for what they did. They are also unable to accept God's forgiveness. They live with a sense of guilt that destroys them and may even cause them to take their own lives due to their inability to be set free from the diabolical knife of self-condemnation. Unforgiveness toward oneself is sin. It locks people in a prison of self-torture, and God hates this.

73

God, in His love, forgives a person all the sins from which he or she sincerely repents. Each person must learn to receive God's forgiveness with a humble heart and thanksgiving. Unforgiveness toward oneself is a sign of great pride and a lack of faith in God's love and mercy. When a person does not forgive him- or herself, that person audaciously takes the position of being higher than God. It's as if that person says, "Even though God forgives me, I will never forgive myself."

If Saul, who in his past had persecuted the Church of Jesus Christ, did not receive God's forgiveness, then he would never have become an apostle and would not have done the things he did. If Peter did not forgive himself for denying his Lord and teacher, then he would have died like Judas. Receiving God's forgiveness is an expression of humility. It's a confession of one's human weaknesses and insignificance and having the understanding of the greatness of God's grace.

Prayer for Forgiving Yourself

Dear heavenly Father! I ask You in the name of Jesus to forgive me for rejecting Your forgiveness. I genuinely repent of this sin against Your love. I believe that You forgave me my sin (name the sin that you couldn't forgive yourself for). Right now, I forgive myself of this sin. I accept Your love and forgiveness and reject all of the Devil's slander against me. Thank You, Jesus, that You are delivering me from my feelings of guilt. Amen."

Resentment toward God

Some people carry resentment in their hearts toward God. There are many reasons that this can happen. Perhaps a person asked something from God and didn't get it, or something terrible happened in the person's life; maybe he or she lost a loved one or was a victim of violence or taunting. Other times, people have questions that disturb them, and they can't find the answers. However, the greatest and most accurate reason for resentment toward God is the Devil's slander. The Devil is a liar and a slanderer. His name reveals the essence of his deeds. He slanders humankind before God, people before each other, men and women against themselves, and people against God. When the thought to blame God enters a person's mind, it is always the work of the Devil.

New believers are not the only ones susceptible to the Devil's influence; great ministers are also just as susceptible. One day Pastor Steve, who was in ministry for many years, received a terrible news. His beloved daughter had perished in an airplane accident. Overwhelming pain, bitterness, and resentment toward God filled his heart so much that he stopped preaching, praying, reading the Bible, and even going to church. This lasted for many months.

Seeing Steve's anguish, God sent another minister named Bob to speak to him. Mr. Bob came in and said, "Give glory to God, or else you will perish." After saying these words, he turned around and left. Steve got down on his knees and tried to squeeze out of himself praise and glory to God for all that had happened. It was as if the Devil was sitting on his shoulder saying, "You are a hypocrite. You know this praise is not in your heart. You are only saying empty words." Steve stopped praying. For fifteen minutes he stood silently, and during this time a battle was raging in his mind and emotions. He opened his mouth again and, through the strength of his will, he made himself praise God. With great effort he forced from himself words of praise and thanksgiving. Within a few minutes he broke through the stubborn fight. His hands flew to heaven, from his mouth poured praise, and his heart overflowed with God's presence. He was truly restored.

God is always good, righteous, and fair. He never makes mistakes and doesn't allow lawlessness. He is able to do everything, including turning what is negative in the life of a person into something good for His glory. A person must repent of his or her sins and the fact that he or she listened to the Devil's slander and then "forgive" God. Then that person will be free to reject all feelings of guilt and give God the glory that He deserves.

Prayer of Repentance
from Resentment toward God

Dear heavenly Father! I ask You in the name of Jesus Christ to forgive me for carrying resentment in my heart toward You because of (name the reason for which you were upset at God). I believed the lies of the Devil—forgive me for this. Right now, I repent of this sin and renounce this slander. I believe that You love me, that You are righteous in Your ways, and that no matter what may happen in my life, You are strong enough to turn it for good in my soul. Thank You, Lord. Amen.

CHAPTER 7

Emotions

When we receive Jesus, God forgives our sins, gladdens our hearts, and becomes one with us. The Holy Spirit now lives in our spirits, but we also have souls. God works on our souls throughout our entire lives on earth. With His Word, God renews our minds so that we can know His will and see all things as God sees them. The Holy Spirit works on our wills, freeing them from all bondage, rebellion, and self-will so that we can willingly obey God's will. God heals and frees our emotions so that we can genuinely rejoice, or when appropriate, cry.

God made humankind to be emotional. He gave us the ability to smile, laugh, rejoice, and cry. The Bible teaches us that we should weep with those who weep and rejoice with those who rejoice (Rom. 12:15). Unfortunately, there are people who never cry, and there are also those who don't know how to rejoice. Such people believe that they were born like this and that they have this type of character, but this way of thinking is all a lie. God did not create them this way; their environment made them this way.

When children are young, they show their emotions easily. If they are hurt or offended, they cry and tears flow from their eyes. If they are having fun and are happy, they rejoice, laugh, and jump around.

Why did God give people tears? Doctors explain that in times of pain, great trial, or sadness, the body manufactures poisons, which are released from the body through tears. If a person holds back tears, then the poisons stay in his or her body and destroy it. People who do not cry become cruel and rude. They can't feel other people's pain, and their hearts become hard as stone. Tears that are provoked by a speck of dust or the aroma of an onion do not contain any poison. For that reason, tears that are provoked by sorrow or inner pain are called bitter tears because they truly are bitter. Adults thrust the false, deceitful assertion that men do not cry on young boys. People who always hold back their tears may, in general, lose the ability to cry.

The deceitful, religious claim that Christians should not laugh and openly express their emotions leads to another extreme. In calling these expressions a manifestation of the flesh, people confuse the flesh with the emotions that are part of the soul. A person who is taught this way regularly suppresses the emotion of joy.

Laughter was created by God. He gave humankind the ability to laugh. God doesn't do anything without a goal and a purpose. Laughter fulfills a definite and important function. Laughter relaxes the nervous system, lowers stress, and leads to a release in the body. The Bible says that a cheerful heart is good medicine, but a crushed spirit dries the bones (Prov. 17:22).

Being cheerful is good for the body and the spiritual life. Emotions allow for internal feelings to come out into the open. Going through grief is shown in the form of crying, tears, sighs, screams, and oftentimes through sobs. Though we should allow our emotions to come out, we must not allow our emotions to control us, and we must not allow our emotions to cause us to go into distress. Feelings of happiness are shown through one's smile, laughter, shouting, clapping, and jumping.

If we observe children, we see that they freely express their emotions even though they are not directly taught how to do this. In observing adults, we very often find that one part of their emotions works poorly, or perhaps a part does not work at all. This malfunction is not due to the absence of emotions, but rather caused by the adults' constant suppression of their feelings.

In the Old and New Testaments, God continually calls His people to live a joyful life. Multiple times in Scripture, it says that Christians should rejoice and be glad. We need to rejoice in times of persecution and in times of sorrow, in times of temptation and in times of suffering. The Bible calls us to rejoice about God, rejoice in God, rejoice with God, and in general, to rejoice always (Matt. 5:11–12; 1 Thess. 5:16; 1 Peter 1:6; 1 Peter 14:13; Ps. 32:1; Phil. 3:1; Phil. 4:4).

Not once in the Scriptures does God reprove His people because they rejoiced too much or too emotionally, especially when it concerns praising Him. It is quite the opposite—God hates despondency, complaining, and unhappiness. God, just like every normal parent, wants and loves to see His children continuously happy and joyful, not crying and despondent.

Children of God who have been washed in the blood of Jesus Christ, who have been saved from hell and eternal judgment, and who have their names written in the Lamb's Book of Life have every reason to live a joyful and happy life. This is why the Bible continually calls upon them to rejoice. A Christian might be sad when praying for dying people, or he or she may cry with those who are going through deep sorrow. A Christian can cry and be sad about sins that he or she committed and come to God in repentance. He or she might be broken and cry, seeking God's face and a closer and deeper relationship with Him. At all other times, however, a Christian should be vivacious. If there is none of this, then there is a reason. It is possible that he or she has spiritual wounds that don't allow the person to be joyful. If a person's heart is wounded, then the joy of others irritates him or her. The person is unable to understand them and to be joyful together with them. This all indicates that he or she is in need of healing.

CHAPTER 8

Healing of
Emotional Wounds

One day, a man went to his pastor and confessed that he had a very serious family problem. Even though he and his wife had already lived together for many years and had children, they had never had a normal, close, friendly relationship. The wife was always irritable and unhappy about something, was constantly finding fault with everything, and was always jealous. When the pastor met with the man's wife, he asked this woman to talk about her life, beginning with her childhood. For a long time she didn't want to talk, as it was very painful for her, but finally she agreed.

The woman had been born into a big family. She had five older sisters. When she was small, her father, whom she loved dearly, died. He was the only one who had truly demonstrated his love to her, and therefore her father's death was a terrible tragedy for the woman. After the death, the woman's mother gave her to her aunt because it was difficult for her to take care of a large family alone. At her aunt's house she cried every night, longing for her father and mother.

When it was time for her to go to school, the woman returned home. Her older sisters constantly yelled at her, laughed at her, and taunted her. They beat and abused her. Her mother was very busy and had never protected her. That's what this woman's childhood was like.

After the woman finished high school, she fled from her sisters and moved to a different state. There she met her future husband. It was a small town, so everyone knew everything about everybody. After she married, she found out about her husband's unpleasant past. They rented her husband's brother's apartment. His brothers also gathered at their apartment, having drinking parties that always ended in scandal. The husband's family constantly insulted this woman, calling her names and putting her down, but her husband never stood up for her. Finally the family left to come to Canada.

The woman's entire past was constantly before her eyes. For this reason she was cold toward her husband and couldn't receive his love. She viewed all of his efforts to love her through a distorted lens. Even his presence annoyed her.

As she told her story, this woman sobbed and wailed. All the pain that was buried in her heart began to come out. She released her father, whom she always longed for, and forgave her sisters, mother, husband, and all of his relatives. After they prayed, her face glowed with happiness. She went home a completely different person.

The same miracle took place in the heart of her husband. His heart had also been consumed with pain. Although he was solid, serious young man, as he shared his story, he cried like a small child. He also went home healed and renewed. Today, this couple is living as an absolutely new family. All the pain of their past has been washed in the blood of Jesus and consigned to oblivion. To this day, they tell everyone about what the great and almighty God can do.

Most often the spiritual wounds people suffer occur during childhood. If these wounds are not healed, people will suffer from them their whole lives. Sometimes no individual is directly responsible for a person's suffering, but whatever the case, spiritual or heart wounds need healing. "Woe is me for my hurt! My wound is severe. But I say, 'Truly this is an infirmity, and I must bear it.' My tent is plundered, and all my cords are broken; my children have gone from me, and they are no more. There is no one to pitch my tent anymore, or set up my curtains" (Jer. 10:19–20).

The death of a dear or beloved person, the loss of a father or mother, a parents' divorce, orphanhood, constant fighting between parents, infidelity, betrayal, rape, the collapse of a family, the loss of children or a close friend, bankruptcy, and rejection are just some of the emotional traumas that leave deep wounds in the heart of a person. These wounds need to be healed.

Some people refuse to accept the death of a loved one. For them, all has grown dark, and life has lost all meaning. Such people lose interest in life and fall into despondency and depression. The Devil convinces them that it is their turn to suffer, since the ones that they loved so much have left them forever.

A certain young man, after burying his beloved wife, was left with five children. He stopped taking care of himself and cast away thoughts of a second marriage. The Devil put him in a cage of loneliness. But when he submitted himself to the will of God and agreed to release his dead wife from his heart, God healed the man's soul. The next day, he came to his friends in a white shirt, and with a smile on his face, said that he intended to find himself a new wife and a mother for his children.

People who have been through a split in their favorite church and traumatized children who have been through their parents' divorce also need healing. If a boy grew up with only his mother or his father, then he didn't receive all that he should have received in a full-fledged family. There are qualities of our characters that only fathers can nurture, and others that only mothers can. That's why God created the whole family to include a father and a mother.

A person must open all areas of his or her life to God so that He can remove, change, fill, and heal the person's heart where needed.

Rejection

Rejection is the most widespread and diseased inner wound. God placed a need to love and be loved into each person. If an individual feels that no one loves or needs him or her, that he or she is unwanted, that he or she is a bother to everyone, that he or she is ugly or inferior, or that no one understands or values him or her, then that person is deprived and suffers greatly. If because of these things he or she doesn't want to live, and has thoughts of suicide, then it means that he or she has experienced strong rejection and needs healing.

There are many reasons that people experience rejection. Sometimes rejection is simply a temporary feeling, and sometimes it brings a spirit that controls a person's whole life. When rejection is in control, it's as if the person wears an invisible stamp that says, "Rejected."

Rejection can even originate at the very moment of conception and development of a child in its mother's womb. As soon as a man and woman's cells unite, a spirit and soul are born. The child matures in the womb not only physically, but also emotionally. Even though the child is still in the womb, his or her spirit and soul are very sensitive. There is an area of the soul that without question should be filled with parents' love. If the child is conceived without the desire of his or her parents, perhaps outside of marriage or in marriage but at an inconvenient time, the child will sense that he or she is not wanted.

There are many reasons parents may not want a pregnancy. Young people may not want to have children immediately, or the wife of a big family may be sick and not want more children. Perhaps the couple believes that any type of family planning is sin, but they continue to be intimate while also praying to God that the timing be off. In the evening they sow, and in the morning they pray that nothing grows, but in spite of their prayers, a pregnancy can result. This news can overwhelm the mother, and she can receive it badly. The child may feel that he or she is not wanted, and instead of feeling love and acceptance, the child will be filled with rejection.

Sometimes parents are hoping for a son and a daughter is born, or the other way around. Either the father or the mother is not happy with the gender of the child. This leads to boys with feminine traits or to girls who acquire male traits, and from these children grow feminine men and manly women. This type of rejection can also lead to homosexual love.

I was once acquainted with a family in which the father only wanted to have sons. He was a gypsy and believed that all daughters are born as another family's merchandise because ultimately they get married and leave their families for another. Despite his wishes, his wife gave birth to a daughter. From her childhood up until she was twelve years old, his daughter behaved like a boy. She played with boys, fought like a boy, climbed trees, and even wore boys' clothing. Her parents were unable to

87

force her into dresses or any other feminine clothing because she would insist that she was a boy and would not wear them. Although she already began to mature as a female, and developed feminine traits, she still rejected the obvious truth and insisted that she was a boy. Eventually, I lost touch with her family, but as long as I knew her, this was what she truly believed.

If a father wants a son, and a daughter is born to him instead, and he does not accept her in his heart, there will be difficulties for a warm and loving relationship between this father and daughter.

Here's another possibility: perhaps the child was wanted and was born, but the parents were too busy or poor so they gave the child to a nursery, a twenty-four-hour daycare, a boarding school, or to an orphanage. Maybe the child's grandmother, grandfather, or babysitter raised him. In these types of situations, the child does not receive his or her parents' love. The child grows with the feeling that his or her parents didn't need the child, and that the child is not wanted.

Sometimes, in the presence of her child, a mother shares with a friend about how hard it was for her to give birth, and how she didn't want the pregnancy. Other times, without thinking, parents tell their children, "Why are you driving me crazy?" or a father may tell his wife in the presence of the children that they are her children, so she needs to raise them. Children interpret these words to mean that their father doesn't need them at all. They feel unwanted and try to find a place to disappear. A mother in a moment of anger may say terrible things, such as, "It would have been better if I had had an abortion." These words, like a sword, pierce the heart of a child, and he may start to think of running away from home, or saying good-bye to life in general.

If parents are harsh and always unhappy, and if they only see the mistakes and shortcomings in their children, then the relationship with their children either closes the children's hearts or stirs them to rebel. The children's feelings of personal worth are destroyed, and they lose their confidence and strength. If a father doesn't display gentleness, tell his children that he loves them, and if he doesn't boast about their successes and hug and kiss them, then a hole is formed in the children's hearts.

Girls who don't receive their parents' love start to look for it outside of the home, often beginning their sexual lives at an early age. These girls don't have sex because they are corrupt or actually want to do this, but because they are seeking love, recognition, and acceptance. Instead of the love that they are seeking, however, their actions lead to even deeper wounds—first they get used, and then they get rejected again.

Boys start committing crimes to be accepted by the crowd. They are ready to do anything that they are told just to be praised. They develop a passion for alcohol and drugs. Sadly, all this is because instead of experiencing love, warmth, and gentleness in their father's home, they experienced rejection.

If a child is not as well-developed as others, had to stay back in school, had some kind of physical or bodily weakness that caused others to laugh at the child or exclude him or her from friendship, then the child is prone to acquiring the spirit of rejection. This is also a strong possibility if he or she was raised in a poor family and had to wear the clothes of his or her older siblings, or if the child's parents dressed him or her unfashionably or got the child a haircut that his or her classmates laughed at.

Rejection may also be a strong possibility if a young person who wanted to get married received a few refusals, if a husband left his wife and found another (or the other way around), or if a girl was raped in her lifetime.

When the spirit of rejection is present, it will accompany a person until the person discovers it and destroys it. In a sense, the person's soul has been branded. No matter what group the person falls into, he or she will be rejected everywhere, and people will do so without even realizing it. Rejected people need acceptance and love very much, but they are not able to receive it or give it to others. They can be very active and generous in church, but they are not motivated by love and compassion for people. Instead, they are motivated by a desire to be noticed, accepted, and recognized.

If a child's parents expected only excellent grades and conduct, and they only praised the child when he or she excelled above all others, then when this child comes to God, he or she will try to do the same to earn God's approval. The child will not be able to understand and receive the unconditional love of God, but instead he or she will always try to please God in order to gain His favor. People who are like this often hate what they do. They are like tethered horses. It is hard for them to believe that God loves them only because they are His children and that they cannot do anything to make Him love them more or less. These people simply need healing, and sometimes they need to be set free from the spirit of rejection.

A certain young man was very active in church. He tried to participate in all the church's activities all the time, but during a time of personal sharing, he tearfully explained that he hated all the things he was doing. He revealed that when he studied in school and brought home a B, his father would ask unhappily, "And why not an A?" From that time on, he decided that he would do better than everyone else, only because he wanted his father to be happy.

There are people who reject themselves because of their outward appearances, finding many faults in themselves. Perhaps they don't like their eyes, ears, mouths, noses, hands, legs, figures, etc. They cannot relate to the words of David when he wrote, "I will praise You, for I am fearfully and wonderfully made" (Ps. 139:14).

Most often, it is girls who suffer from self-rejection. In spite of their negative opinions of themselves, however, others see these girls as beautiful. The Devil deceives them, and as a result many girls suffer feelings of inferiority and low self-worth. They need to reject this lie of the Devil and believe that even before their births, God had a plan for them. In His plan, He also designed their external appearance. It was God's hands that wove these girls in the womb of their mothers. They are original and unique. He likes and is pleased with these young ladies exactly the way they are, and without question there is a young man for each young lady who will love her exactly as she looks because he finds her attractive.

There are no ugly people, just as there are no ugly flowers. Each person is beautiful and original in his or her own way. Sin, sorrow, bitterness, and unhappiness deprive a person of beauty and attractiveness. Someone said that the ugliest woman is an evil woman. To this might be added that a happy and joyful person cannot be ugly even if he or she has a physical defect. What we may define as a defect does not decrease a person's originality or attractiveness.

If a person has experienced rejection from others, he or she must forgive those who have hurt him or her, renounce his or her negative feelings, and receive the complete healing of his or her emotions. The person must renew his or her thoughts with God's Word, and the person's life will be changed. The rejected soul will then see that he or she is genuinely loved and that he or she is not unwanted in his or her family, in the church, or on this earth. Through Jesus Christ's sacrifice, there is healing from all forms of rejection. He was rejected by this earth and left by His heavenly Father so that every person would be accepted into God's family and have the opportunity to enjoy His love.

Prayer

Dear heavenly Father! I thank You that You chose me through Jesus Christ even before the foundation of the earth. Your hands wove me in the womb of my mother. I believe that I was not accidentally born to this earth. I today forgive all the people that rejected me and caused me pain (name all the people that rejected you and in what specific way). I forgive them with all my heart, love them, and bless them. I renounce all rejection and proclaim that I am chosen, loved, and accepted by my heavenly Father. I am unique, beautiful, and irreplaceable. Lord, heal the wounds that people have caused me when they knowingly or unknowingly rejected me. I accept Your healing love right now and thank You in the name of Jesus Christ. Thank You, Lord. Amen.

Shyness

Some people have been labeled as shy. There are those who think that being shy is normal and consider this quality as being one of the virtues. This, however, it is not true. Modesty and shamefulness are virtues, but shyness is bondage.

A shy person is one who is ashamed of him- or herself. The reason for this might be pride, low self-worth, or fear of others' opinions. The shy person is too worried about what others think of him or her, is afraid to look bad in public, and afraid of that people will think or say about him or her. This prevents the person from being him- or herself and doing what the person needs to do in certain situations.

Shy people are afraid to sing, pray out loud, raise their hands to God, shout to God, loudly praise Him, and testify about Him. They cannot speak when asked to do so or when situations demand. They are afraid to express their emotions because fear and dependence on the opinions of others bind them.

If blind Bartholomew had been shy, he would have died blind. If the woman who suffered with from a blood disorder had been shy, she would have died from her illness. If Zac-chae'us had been shy, he never would have been saved. If Jesus had been shy, He never would have gone to the cross because the cross is a place of shame.

Shyness is a form of bondage that prevents people from entering their calling and fulfilling the will of God. Service to God is always associated with risk. A person striving for a goal will without fail make mistakes. He or she will have to go against the opinion of the crowd more than once. He or she will need to be brave to confess his or her mistakes and ask forgiveness of other people. Shyness doesn't lend itself to heroic deeds.

What separates modesty and shamefulness from shyness? Modesty is when a person limits him- or herself for the sake and good of others. It can be expressed in such things as clothing, eating, fellowship, and speaking. Shamefulness is when a person, acting in the fear of God, hides his or her nakedness and doesn't display it for general view. Shyness is when a person limits him- or herself without a reason, acting in fear of the opinions of others.

A shy person has a hard time believing in Jesus because God's opinions are very often different from the opinions of people. Jesus said, "How can you believe, who receive honor from one another, and do not seek the honor that comes from the only God?" (John 5:44)

The blows of life, the ridicule of people, and the failures and mistakes of the past can make people shy. Those who are shy need to have their minds renewed, their emotions healed, and their lives set free from fearing the opinions of others.

A middle-aged man was afraid to speak in front of a big auditorium of people. He didn't know the cause of his fear. When his pastor ministered to him, the Holy Spirit very clearly showed him an event in his life that he had long forgotten about. This moment was in China when the man was thirteen. There were underground churches, and Christians met in private homes for their services. One of the Christians at the meeting suggested that the man sit beside him. He obediently sat down, not suspecting anything.

When the meeting started, the leader who was in charge said, "Today a young preacher will read for us." As he said this, he presented the young man with a Bible and put him before the gathering. The poor man's throat went dry, his hands shook, and his legs almost gave out. Struck with fear and worry, he couldn't say one word. In shame, he rushed outside and ran away and afterward avoided seeing that minister. He was seized with a fear of speaking before crowds and became embarrassed. When he was finally able to forgive this minister, the power of fear was broken in his life, and he began to speak freely before large auditoriums of people.

If a person dreams of having a genuine ministry for God, he or she needs to be set free from the vice of shyness.

CHAPTER 9

False Names
and Predictions

The God we serve has many different names, which all define His being. In making His names known to people, God also revealed His character. The following is a list of just a few of God's names:

- ❑ Jehovah: Existing, having life in Himself
- ❑ Jehovah Raffa: The Lord, my Healer
- ❑ Jehovah Nissi: The Lord, my banner
- ❑ Jehovah Roffi: The Lord, my Shepherd

When a person is born, he or she is given a name. Children may be named in honor of another person, or simply because the parents like a certain name. Few people actually think about what names mean, but each name has its own sense and meaning. In ancient times, people gave their children names associated with a particular event, a physical trait, or the character of the child.

To great misfortune, during the course of life, and especially in childhood, people pick up different, unofficial names. They get these names most often from their parents. Such names usually have negative meanings and cling to children like labels.

It's likely that each person has heard or has been called one or more of the following names: dunce, dimwit, slob, sluggard, blockhead, fool, weakling, lame, idiot, wimp, nutcake, slacker, ninny, oddball, failure, poor student, and other negative words of this sort. Some have heard names that are even more harsh and offensive. From the things you hear in the discussions and conversations of families, some homes seem more like farms than families. People call each other pigs, goats, donkeys, oxen, cows, dogs, cattle, and other livestock. You rarely hear children being addressed with gentle, warm words.

It's hard to understand why the parents described in 1 Kings 25 named their son Nabal, which means "folly." The child was called this not because he was stupid, but he ended up becoming foolish because of the name that he was called throughout life. Eventually his stupidity and his stupid deeds led to his death.

Parents are rarely aware that the names and nicknames that they give their children form the thoughts of their children and determine the direction of their lives. Usually by giving their children negative names and speaking negative things, parents predict a negative future for them:

- ❏ You will never have any money.
- ❏ You will be paying off your debt your entire life.
- ❏ You will beg your whole life.
- ❏ You will never get married.
- ❏ You will clean toilets for a living.
- ❏ You will be a fast-food worker for a living.
- ❏ Nothing will work out for you.
- ❏ You won't get anywhere in life.
- ❏ Only prison can change you now.
- ❏ You will never amount to anything.
- ❏ Nothing good will ever come of your life.

The Bible says that life and death are in the power of the tongue (Prov. 18:22). Our tongues play a role in our lives similar to the wheel of a ship or the bridle of a horse.

The confession of the mouth influences the direction of a person's life (James 3:3–4). For example, as he or she grows older, a person who has been a victim of harsh words may ask in surprise, "How did my parents know that my life would turn out this way?" Such a person has come to a false conclusion about the root cause of his or her problems. The negative things have happened to this person because his or her parents, or someone else who had authority over this person, spoke them into his or her life.

Sometimes people say things without even thinking about them. Theologians claim that over 80 percent of the words that people speak have negative meanings. Here are a few examples:

- ❑ Better to die than to live like this.
- ❑ Better not to have children at all than to have these kids.
- ❑ Better not to work at all than to work this way.
- ❑ Better not to do anything at all than to do this.
- ❑ Don't go out without your coat, or you will get sick.
- ❑ Don't drive fast, or you will get in an accident.
- ❑ Don't be friends with them, or you will end up in prison.
- ❑ Small children won't let you sleep, and big children won't let you live.
- ❑ Small children, small problems; big children, big problems.

People come to a point when they want to know the source of the problems and havoc that is in their lives and in the lives of their children. The answer is simple—words are like seeds, as Jesus said (Mark 4:14). All words have authority and power, whether they come from the Bible or are just general, everyday words. An individual is either justified or judged by his or her words (Matt. 12:36–37). There comes a time when the word that is sown brings forth its harvest.

One Christian father, when talking about his children, said, "I'm raising bandits." He didn't put any special weight on his words, but his children eventually grew up to be criminals.

Isn't it better to speak as Joshua spoke when he said that he and his house would serve the Lord? Jacob's life was marked by a terrible tragedy when one day his sons returned home with the bloody clothing of his beloved son. This was a serious blow to him. "Then Jacob tore his clothes, put sackcloth on and mourned for his son many days. And all his sons and daughters arose to comfort him; but he refused to be comforted, and he said, 'For I shall go down into the grave to my son in mourning.' Thus his father wept for him" (Gen. 37:34–35).

With these words, Jacob condemned himself to a sorrowful life, through which he lived for twenty-two years. When his sons returned from Egypt one day and announced that Joseph was alive and ruling over Egypt, Jacob didn't believe them, but instead became troubled (Gen. 45:26). Only after his sons told him more details and showed him Joseph's chariots did Jacob's soul revive, so he said, "Enough." What did he mean when he said this? He meant that he had had enough mourning. "I will go and see him," he said.

In similar ways, people bind themselves with their own words, condemning their lives to a pitiful existence and to loneliness, poverty, failure, and sadness. Frequently the people of Israel told God that they wouldn't enter the Promised Land, and finally one day God told Moses: "Say to them, 'As I live,' says the Lord, 'just as you have spoken in My hearing, so I will do to you: The carcasses of you

101

who have complained against Me shall all in this wilderness, all of you who were numbered, according to your entire number, from twenty years old and above ... You shall by no means enter the land which I swore I would make you dwell in'" (Num. 14:28–30).

The Israelites were prevented from entering the Promised Land not because God didn't want to take them there, but because they didn't believe His promises, and they uttered their doubts out loud.

As I have ministered to people, I have been frequently convinced of how often the life of a person corresponds to words that have been spoken over him or her. One day, a young man came to me in pain. "Pastor, I will never be able to get married. I ask young women to marry me, and they always refuse. The last time it happened, I was turned down just before the wedding. I am tired of this and don't know what to do." I asked him, "Have you said anything in the past about marriage?" He answered, "I said that I would not get married before the age of thirty." At that time he was only twenty-five.

Another woman tearfully told me, "My father always said that I would clean toilets my entire life. That's exactly what I am doing now."

An old woman used to date one man when she was young. She decided to end her relationship with him, and she looked for any possible reason to do so. Once, when they were on a date, she said that she no longer wanted to be in a relationship with him, so he started to ask her about her reasoning. She said that she had been told that he had another woman and two children. She knew it was a lie. The young man said that that was lie and that he didn't have any relationships with anyone other than her. After this argument, they went their separate ways. Many years went by, and this woman got married to another man. They lived together for many terrible years. One day a young woman came to her and said, "I have been acquainted with your husband for a long time. We love each other, and I have two children with him." With her own leaps, she created her own fate.

There is no end to these types of stories. Is there a way to avoid them? Of course there is. God has not planned a broken destiny for any person. "For I know the thoughts that I think toward you, say the Lord, thoughts of peace and not of evil, plans to give you a future and a hope" (Jer. 29:11).

Jesus said that He came so that we would have life and have it abundantly (John 10:10).

God opted for health, the salvation of families, successful marriages, orderliness, creativity, blessings, success, and protection for His children. The Devil, however, tries to throw his fate at them through the presence of their negative words. When voicing incorrect thoughts, a person allows the Devil to invade his or her life in exactly the area of which he or she speaks. The Devil will go as far as each person allows him to go. A person allows this to happen either through his or her spoken words or through his or her fears, which is also a type of faith, but a negative one.

In order for a person's life to change, it is necessary for him or her to promptly reject all the labels and negative words that either he or she or someone else has spoken over his or her life. Before Abraham was the father of many nations, God changed his name from Abram (great father) to Abraham (the father of many). Before Jacob's life changed, God changed his name. His former name, Jacob, meaning stammerer or cunning, became Israel, meaning God's hero or God's king. Before the heart of Simon Barjona was changed, Jesus gave him the new name Peter, meaning stone.

Before a sinner begins to live a righteous life, he or she needs to change his or her name to "righteous one." Before a lawless one begins to live a holy life, he or she needs to change his or her name to "holy." In order to live a victorious life, you need to be called a victor. First change the name and then change the conduct and the way of life. At the moment of their repentance, God gives all of His children new names. All those who are Christians should refer to themselves and all the people around them the way that God speaks about them in His Word. What a person sees or feels is not important. What is important is what God speaks. This trust in God's Word is the kind of genuine faith that determines the course of a person's life.

Prayer

Dear Lord! Forgive me for all the negative words that I spoke into my life (list all of the negative words that you spoke). I repent in this and renounce all of these words. In the name of Jesus Christ, I rid them of all power and authority over my life. I forgive everyone that also spoke negative things into my life (list all things, that other people spoke). I don't believe in these words. I renounce them and rid them of all power and authority in my life. Lord, I believe in everything that You spoke toward me in Your Word (proclaim positive words over your life in place of the negative ones).

CHAPTER 10

Judgment and Decisions
of the Heart

J esus taught us, "Judge not, and you shall not be judged. Condemn not, and you shall not be condemned. Forgive, and you will be forgiven" (Luke 6:37).

This Scripture tells us that if a person judges someone for a sin or an improper action, then there will come a time when that person will also be judged, and possibly for the very same thing. Sometimes in judging other people, a person may say:

"How could that person do that? I would never do that ..."

"I will never do what that person did ..."

"I will never be the same as ..."

"I will never have as disobedient children as ..."

"I will never be in debt like ..."

People make many other similar promises, either verbally or in their hearts. The time will come when they will mature and suddenly discover that they did the very same deeds for which they judged other people; or they may stay true to their words, but it'll never work for their benefit. Why does this happen?

Firstly, when a person judges another, he or she sows something negative into his or her life. Secondly, a person who judges trusts in him- or herself and in his or her flesh, essentially proclaiming, "I am different and better, and that's why I will never do such a thing!" The Bible says that cursed is the person who trusts in his or her own flesh (Jer. 17:5). This type of trust gives the Devil legal right to a specific area of a person's life. The Devil is well versed in the law, and if you give him a chance, he will always use it against you. "Do not let your mouth cause your flesh to sin, nor say before the messenger of God that it was an error. Why should God be angry at your excuse and destroy the work of your hands?" (Eccl. 5:6).

A person's inward decisions usually sprout from the soil of his or her judgment of others and from unforgiveness, especially when he or she has been a victim. If, for example, a child was harshly punished in childhood and then decided that he or she would never beat his or her children, there is a good chance that child will do the same, or maybe even worse than his or her parents did. Or the opposite may also happen; the child may not discipline his or her children at all, even though they may very much need it. If a child grew up in a big family and suffered greatly because of this, then the child may decide that he or she will never have a big family. As a result of that person's decision, maybe he or she will not be able to have children at all. That person may end up having a problem with his or her health in the area of fertility.

One young son hated his father because he was always drunk. When the father returned home drunk after work, the son was ashamed to admit to his friends that this was his father so the son decided that he would never drink like that. When his father died, however, the son became a bitter drunk, even worse than his father had been. The son came to God and repented, but still he continued to crave alcohol. When the man forgave his father, repented for judging him, and renounced the curse that he had received in childhood, God fully set him free from this vice.

A woman grew up in a large family. Her father led a depraved lifestyle, and all of the children suffered because of it. The woman's mother, however, loved her father very much and forgave him everything. As a child, this woman decided never to marry a man that she really loved because she didn't want to turn out like her mother. When she grew up, a man that she loved proposed to her. In spite of her strong feelings, she turned him down and married a man she didn't really love. As a result, she was never happy in her marriage until the time that she repented for judging her mother and making her childhood marriage decision. From the moment that she renounced this sin, her marriage began to improve.

A small child told his mother his childhood secret and accidentally, the mother told her friend about it. The son heard her share his secret, was greatly offended, and decided never to tell women secrets. After a while, he grew up and got married. There were always problems in his family because he wouldn't tell his wife anything, not even general things. This lack of communication continued to make a hole in their marriage until God showed this man the root of his problem. When the root was torn out, the man became open, vulnerable, and trusting.

One girl had strong feelings of hate toward all pregnant women. She said that she would never carry the child in the front, but would carry it in the back. She got married, and they had no children. Her husband was paralyzed, and during her entire life, she had to carry him on her back.

Another young woman condemned her mother for leaving them when they were still young. When she grew older, she got married and had children. Once, in a very critical situation, she left her children in the car and ran away. They were in the car for many hours by themselves. Everything turned out all right, but she was still unable to forgive herself for leaving her children.

Sometimes people proclaim, "I will never set foot in your home again." We also hear the expression, "Over my dead body." There was a family in which the father and children really wanted to move to another state, but the mother said, "Over my dead body!" The family did move, but before they did so, they also buried their mother.

In order for a person's life to be changed, he or she must repent of all the judgment that resides in his or her heart and forgive all the people who caused that person to make those judgments. The person must also renounce all inner curses and release his or her authority over his or her life. Next, the person must submit to the will of God and fully trust in His almighty grace. In following these steps, a person is able to turn all the negative things in his or her life around for good.

Prayer

Dear Lord! I ask You in the name of Jesus Christ to forgive me for my condemnation of people and the oaths that I have made in my heart. I repent in the sin of condemnation and renounce of all the oaths that I made while relying on myself and my own strength (list all of the moments of condemnation and internal decisions). Lord, deliver me from all of the negative consequences of these convictions, and may all these oaths be destroyed. I renounce any dependence of myself. I ask You to help me to not become the very things I condemned people for. I solely rely on You and Your grace. Thank You, Lord. Amen.

CHAPTER 11

Negative Expectations

Some people's lives, or the lives of their relatives, are characterized by a tendency to always expect the worst. If they had colds for two autumns in a row, then when the third autumn comes around, they are already expecting to catch a cold. In the spring, this type of person anticipates allergies, since he or she has them in the previous year. This kind of thinking leads people to easily accept all sorts of illnesses and problems, and consequently, they become a part of their lives.

The Bible says that faith is the substance of things hoped for (Heb. 11:1). The law of faith works with both positive and negative thoughts. If an individual believes and waits for something, then there is a very good chance that it will happen. Every Christian should believe in the Word of God and what is written in it. He or she should not agree with what he or she sees and feels, but with what God's Word says. That doesn't mean that he or she should reject absolutely everything, but rather that the person should not resign him- or herself to problems that don't actually exist.

People are often quick to accept crumbs from the Devil in the form of sickness, allergies, insomnia, and even death. The Devil is a liar and a deceiver. He can cause a person to experience symptoms of all types of diseases, and if a person accepts these symptoms as an actual illness, then the illness will follow. A Christian should defend his or her health and fight for it.

There was a woman who began to have pain in her breast, so she went to get checked by the doctor. They did an x-ray and said that she had cancer and that they needed to operate immediately. The woman said it was impossible that she had cancer and that she would not let them operate on her. The doctors tried to convince her, showing her the x-ray with the tumor. She replied by saying that maybe the tumor was on the x-ray, but it wasn't in her. Seeing that it was useless to argue, her doctor let her go home and told her to come back in a few weeks. The doctor figured that the illness would reveal itself to her over time and that she would come back even sooner than her next appointment. The woman returned as originally scheduled. The doctors did another x-ray, but couldn't find anything. They examined her again and again found nothing. The amazed doctors began to apologize, and the woman quietly went home victorious. She is healthy and alive to this day.

There are people who have seen early death or divorce in the lives of their relatives, or how an acquaintance's children became worldly or addicted to drugs. These people go on to live with the fear that soon the same thing will happen in their lives.

A person may battle with a certain sin and continuously endure shame. He or she has lost so much faith through failing to have control over his or her sin that even before the person repents for the habitual sin, the person knows that his or her repentance is temporary and that he or she will fall into sin again. And of course, because the person anticipates it, he or she does fall.

The Bible teaches us to walk in faith and not by sight. This means that we build our lives not on the foundation of what we see, hear, and feel but on the foundation of what God says in His Word. The Devil always paints a picture of a future filled with failure, shame, sickness, lost children, divorced families, early death, and other negative things. Additionally, he can frighten people with superstitions, such as sprinkled salt, a black cat, broken mirrors, and so on. When people accept these lies of the Devil, they allow him to invade their lives and bring destruction.

What a person believes determines what will control him or her. Those in whom a person believes in are those in whom he or she will trust. Those in whom a person trusts are those whom a person will allow into his or her life.

The Psalm 90 is known as the psalm of protection. Both believers and nonbelievers use it. The nineth verse is the central verse. "Because you have made the Lord, who is my refuge, even the Most High, your dwelling place ..." (Ps. 91:9).

These words explain why the Lord values, keeps, covers, helps, and protects you. It describes the perspective of one who understands where best to put his trust. It is not in the life you had before, what is around you now, and what others have. It is in knowing who your refuge is and what God says about you.

A man bought a medical encyclopedia in which there were described various illnesses and their symptoms. When he began to read it, something began to happen to him. One thing began to hurt, then a second thing, then a third. He began to discover symptoms that he didn't have before. Terrified, the man ran to a pastor and told him that everything in his body hurt. He asked the pastor to pray so that God would heal him. The pastor told him, "Stop reading the encyclopedia and start reading the Bible, and immediately you will be healed."

> Whose report will you believe?
> I will believe the report of the Lord.
> Jesus Christ said I am saved,
> Jesus Christ said I am healed,
> Jesus Christ said I am free,
> Jesus bought my victory!

We all need to examine ourselves—is there something in our minds that the Devil could bind us with, or something that we would accept without a fight? Symptoms don't necessarily mean sickness. Faith in God as the healer sets us free from all symptoms and illnesses. By trusting in God, people of faith wait for the salvation of their homes, the strengthening of their marriages, long lives, good health, victory over sin and temptation, and all the goodness that God keeps for those who fear Him. People of faith do not expect shame; they have the conqueror. They don't expect sickness; they have the healer. People of faith don't expect poverty; they have the provider. They don't expect an untimely death; they have the one who Himself is the resurrection and the life.

People of faith don't sing this song:

> Will I really make it, my God?
> When You come for Your own,
> Will I remain here in torment?
> And You will not take me home?

But they proclaim confidently:

> Soon it will be the dawn of a new day;
>   spring is coming.
> I see Him as He is; yes, He is coming to meet me.
> Coming in glory, I wait for Him.
> I am waiting for the Lord, Your coming.

> Come! We are Your people, and
> We have left all behind, and
> You go before us in the clouds to meet us.

115

With You, we will go to heaven and in peace.
Open the door and go home.
Returning to our Father's home—
Come!

Reject all negative expectations, and receive the blessed and happy destiny of the loving God.

CHAPTER 12

Curse

The topic of curse produces many questions and differing opinions among Christians. Through a careful study of the Word of God, one can discover that there is quite a lot written on this subject. Blessing and curse are like the spiritual laws of sowing and reaping. That which a person sows, he or she will reap. This law has worked since the foundation of the earth, and it has not changed.

From the very first chapter of the book of Genesis, we are introduced to blessings, and the third chapter speaks of how curse came to the earth. Curse is the consequence or retribution of sin that mankind inherits while on earth. Because of the sin of Adam, the earth was cursed. It began to bring forth thorns and thistles. Since the time of Adam, people have had to work by the sweat of their brows to get something good to grow out of the earth (Gen. 3:17–19).

The earth cursed Cain, the first son of Adam and Eve, because it had received the blood of his brother Abel, whom he murdered. The earth stopped bringing forth fruit when Cain cultivated it, so from then on, Cain could no longer live peaceably on earth. The earth rejected him, and wandering became his fate and punishment (Gen. 4:11–12).

Righteous Noah, having lived through the flood, cursed Canaan, the son of Ham. Ham looked without shame upon the nakedness of his father, Noah, and then laughingly told his brothers about it. As a result, Canaan was condemned to always be a servant to his brothers (Gen. 9:25).

When God called Abraham, He told him, "I will bless those who bless you, and I will curse him who curses you" (Gen. 12:3).

So even before the law, curse was working in the land. With the coming of the law, the curse of the law increased. When Israel entered the Promised Land, six tribes were to stand on the mountain of Gerizim to bless the people, and six were to stand on the mountain of Ebal to proclaim curse.

Blessings and curses were the outcome of specific relationships with God's laws. If you fulfilled the law, you were blessed; if you broke it, you were cursed. The chapters 27 and 28 of Deuteronomy speak in detail about this. Four times as many references to curses are made there compared to blessings.

Things that lead to curse

1. Idolatry (witchcraft and all that is associated with the occult)
2. Speaking disrespectfully to parents

3. Improper attitude toward others in regard to property (e.g., intrusion of borders)
4. Improper attitude toward with the disabled and sick (e.g., knocking down the blind who are in the way)
5. Improper attitudes toward the weak and defenseless (e.g., improper judgment and oppression of newcomers, widows, and orphans)
6. Incest (sexual relations with close relatives)
7. Bestiality (sexual relations with animals)
9. Murder
9. Paying someone for murder
10. Not fulfilling the law
11. Not serving God with a glad and happy heart
12. Loss of the fear of God
13. Hope in humankind and self-sufficiency (Jer. 17:5)
14. Robbery (Zach. 5:3)
15. Not giving a tithe (Mal. 3:9)
16. Cheating in marriage (Num. 5:27)

Curse affects all the areas of a person's life

1. Coming and going
2. Field and flock
3. Family and children
4. Business and work

5. Health and success
6. War and money
7. Abiding in the Promised Land

To put it simply, curse is the absence of blessing. It occurs when there is continual shame and failure in a particular area of a person's life. Instead of building, there is destruction; instead of health, there is sickness; instead of abundance, there is debt; instead of fruitfulness, there is barrenness; instead of peace and rest, there is nervousness, worry, and fear.

Does curse exist today? As long as we live on a cursed land, curse will exist. Today, as in the past, the earth continues to bring forth thorns, and women continue to bear their children with great pain. Only in the new heaven and in the new earth will there be no more curses. "And there shall be no more curse ..." (Rev. 22:3).

Redemption from Curses

Through the disobedience of Adam, sin came into the earth, and through sin came death. Through inheritance or genetics, sin passes to all people (Rom. 5:12). Sin did not come alone, but the consequences are:

1. Separation from God
2. Guilt and judgment

3. Sickness
4. Poverty
5. Shame
6. Destruction
7. Bondage
8. Curses
9. Demonic possession
10. Death
11. Eternal judgment

Jesus came to set humankind free from sin and all of its consequences. Sin is the same in the Old Testament and in the New Testament, and what it brought with it in the Old Testament, it brings with it into the New Testament as well. "Then, when desire has conceived, it gives birth to sin; and sin, when it is full-grown, gives forth death" (James 1:15).

Sin is an open door for the Devil, giving him rights in specific areas of a person's life.

Curses are one of the wages of sin. We already said that on the cross of Calvary, Jesus took upon Himself all sin and all curse. Through His death, He redeemed us from the oath of the law. He, who is in Christ, is no longer under the law (Rom. 6:14).

On the cross an exchange took place. Jesus took upon Himself that which we deserved and gave us that which He deserved. According to the foundation of the law, those who fulfilled it fully were blessed, and those who broke any part of it were cursed. We all broke the law, and Jesus fulfilled it all. Based on the law, we all deserved to be cursed, and Jesus deserved blessing. He took upon Himself our curse and gave us His blessings. He fulfilled the law in order to redeem those who were under the law (Gal. 4:4–5).

The law gave authority to sin and produced curse.

> For apart from the law sin was dead. (Rom. 7:8)

> So that sin through the commandment might become exceedingly sinful. (Rom. 7:13)

> Christ redeemed us from the curse of the law, having become a curse for us. (Gal. 3:13)

Jesus, therefore, redeemed us from sin, the law, and the curse of the law. Redemption and salvation are 100 percent complete. God's work has been perfected once and for all, and it has been perfected for absolutely everyone. Salvation is a complete package, and it includes everything that a person needs.

When an individual receives Christ into his or her heart, that person receives all that salvation includes: salvation from sin, freedom from sickness, weakness, poverty, the law, cursings, guilt, judgment, rejection, Adam's sinful nature, this world, this century, demonic authority, and deliverance from the fear of death, hell, and eternal perdition. A person already has the potential for this freedom within him- or herself, but he or she must now possess it in a practical sense.

Before the people of Israel entered the Promised Land, God said that the land already belonged to them. This is why He gave them the command to fight and take possession of it. Legally, the land belonged to Israel, but in a practical sense, it belonged to the people of Canaan. It was necessary for the people of Israel to fight to possess the land that already belonged to them. This is the way all other things also work in God's kingdom.

On the cross, Jesus obtained everything for us. The moment we repent, we receive this complete victory, even though we still don't clearly understand what we are receiving. After repentance, as we begin to live our new lives, the Holy Spirit uses revelations to make this victory become real to us. "However, when he, the Spirit of truth, has come, He will guide you into all truth; for He will not speak on His own authority, but whatever He hears He will speak; and He will tell you things to come. He will glorify Me, for He will take what is Mine and declare it to you" (John 16:13–14).

Curse was destroyed two thousand years ago on the cross in the same way that sin was destroyed. It remains up to us to receive this victory into our lives by faith. Receiving Christ's victory now depends solely on humankind—will we really possess it or not? This decision involves forgiveness, healing, deliverance, and blessings. Nothing happens in God's kingdom automatically.

God doesn't want His children to experience only a small portion of His salvation, but He desires that His children delight in all the fullness of His riches. Many Christians speak as if they know only victory, but they live in constant defeat. They speak of freedom, but they live in the slavery of sin, lust, and bad habits. They speak of blessing, but their lives are full of curse. Like an ostrich that hides its head in the sand, they close their eyes to the things that shouldn't be in their lives and pretend that all is well. It's time to open our eyes and enter into God's light.

Special Types of Curse

Curse always enters a person's life for a reason. This might be because of a person's own sin or the sin of his or her forefathers. Cain's life was cursed because of his own guilt. Not only did he suffer because of this curse, but his children did also. It was not Canaan's guilt that caused his grandfather, Noah, to curse him. Canaan's father, Ham, sinned, and his curse was passed to Canaan and all of his descendants. As a consequence, when the people of Israel arrived in the Promised Land, they were supposed to destroy all the people who were descendents of Canaan.

When the Jewish people stood before Pilate and demanded the death of Jesus, they proclaimed a curse upon themselves and upon their children. For two thousand years, this curse has been upon these people. In spite of the fact that they are God's chosen and blessed people, they are under the law of curse, a law that they themselves proclaimed over their own lives.

We see that curses are not limited to one person, but that they may be passed from generation to generation. Even people who experience blessings may experience curse in a specific area of their lives. In many areas of their lives, everything may be normal, but in other areas, it seems like an unseen power continually brings about destruction.

One day, David, the blessed king of Israel, committed murder and adultery. Even though God forgave him for this sin, there was still great retribution. First David's son, who was conceived in sin, died. Then David's sin began to appear in the lives of his children. His son, Amnon, raped his daughter, Tamar. Another son, Absalom, killed Amnon because of what he had done to his sister. Absalom then went to war against his father, committed adultery with all the wives of the king, and in the end, died in shame. Through his sin, David opened the door to curse in his personal life and in the lives of his children. His children began to do openly that which their father had done in secret. In spite of this tragedy, David remained a blessed king.

The sins, negative habits, character, and various weaknesses of parents can be passed down as an inheritance to their children. Blessed Abraham, out of fear for his own life, twice allowed his wife Sarah to be seized by different kings. Only thanks to God's mercy and faithfulness was she spared from harm. Abraham's son Isaac, who wasn't even born at that time of his father's sins and couldn't have known about them, repeated the same sin with his wife Rebecca (Gen. 12:11–20, 20:1–18, 26:7–11).

God, in revealing His name to Moses, proclaimed, "The Lord, the Lord God, merciful and gracious, longsuffering, and abounding in goodness and truth, keeping mercy for thousands, forgiving iniquity and transgression and sin, by no means clearing the guilty, visiting the iniquity of the fathers upon the children and the children's children to the third and the fourth generation" (Ex. 34:6–7).

God's nature and character never change. He is the same yesterday, today and forever. His mercy and punishment for sin run simultaneously. His punishment of parents' guilt extends to their children, and this influence may be seen to even the third and forth generations; the sin of a father or mother can be passed to his or her children, and in turn, the punishment for that sin may also be passed to the children's children. Four generations is approximately two hundred years and includes thirty descendants.

Illnesses can also be passed down by inheritance. When we go to the doctor for an appointment, we need to fill out a certain type of questionnaire. It has many questions regarding the illnesses of our parents and grandparents. Why do doctors ask us about these things? Because there is a good chance that we could inherit these same types of problems. The questionnaire is the same for everyone, believers and nonbelievers.

Glory to God, who, with His blood, came to save us from the vanities of life and from the sins, curses, sicknesses, and weaknesses that are passed down to us from our fathers. He also redeemed us from all curses that we may bring upon ourselves. All we need to do is to expose these curses, repent from them, and destroy their authority over our lives and the lives of our children.

Key signs in the presence of curse:

1. Mental illness
2. Physical disorders
3. Ulcers and chronic illnesses
4. Constant debt and poverty
5. Frequent accidents
6. Inherited illnesses
7. Inherited sins and vices
8. Infertility
9. Miscarriages
10. Frequent depression
11. Constant failure
12. Tendency toward accidents and mishaps
13. Divorce and ruined marriages
14. Reoccurring early deaths in a family
15. Suicides in a family
16. Constant disappointment
17. Generational prostitution

Key causes for the occurrence of curses:

1. Idolatry, fortune telling, witchcraft, sorcery, and occultism
2. Sexual sin and immoral lifestyle
3. Disobedience toward parents; disrespect toward parents
4. Stealing
5. Unfairness toward those who are weak
6. Mockery of the disabled and the sick
7. Murder and abortion
8. Anti-Semitism and denigration of Jews
9. Hope and reliance on one's own flesh
10. Cruelty toward animals
11. Elders cursing those who are younger
12. Serving those who pronounce curses
13. Curses called or spoken by witches or occultists
14. Taking and/or not fulfilling a pronounced oath
15. Curses directed against oneself

Transferred Curses

The primary bearers of curses are the words spoken by a person. We have already said that life and death are in the power of the tongue. With the tongue, we can bless God and curse people (James 3:9). Undeserved curses do not have power, but deserved ones do. If a person steals something, and owner of this thing curses him or her, even if the owner doesn't see the thief, that curse might affect the thief's life.

There was a man who constantly offended his wife, and it hurt her so much that she wished that he would break his back. Not long after, as he was climbing the stairs, the staircase collapsed, and he broke his back.

Parents often speak multiple curses into the lives of their children. Over time, those curses come to pass. Others speak negatively about themselves, and those words also become true. People curse murderers, rapists, and robbers, as well as their descendants, and all of those curses eventually manifest in the lives of these people.

A Christian man had a child with stunted development. It turns out that as a child, this man and his friends laughed at and made fun of a woman with a nervous disorder. She cursed them and, as they grew older, the same type of illness afflicted their children.

Curse-bearers can also be occult objects, good luck charms, sacred cards, photographs, occult books, and films. In the book of Acts, an event that took place in Ephesus is described. The people of that city turned to God, and those who were involved in sorcery confessed their sins and burned all of their occult books (Acts 19:18–20).

A woman used to have a portrait of her grandmother in her bedroom. The woman's children had trouble sleeping in the room where the photo was located. It turned out that the woman's grandmother was a witch, so when a pastor ministered to the woman and began to break the curses coming from the photo, the woman began to demonstrate demonic manifestations. The portrait was destroyed, the curse was broken, and the woman received total deliverance. After that her children began to sleep well.

Curse can be borne by tattooing various signs, dragons, and letters on the body. There can be curses upon a house, building, or piece of land. There are homes that are consecrated to satanic rituals, and because of this, night spirits and "drummers" live there. People cannot live in these homes because at nighttime someone bangs the kitchen dishes and cupboard doors.

Witches and other occult healers use a wide assortment of tools such as needles, hair, photographs, bones, clothes, liquids, blood, and so on. Very often behind their spells are demonic curses that have the power to destroy a person's life.

Every curse should be brought to light through confession, and there should be complete repentance for the sin that allowed the curse to come. Only after these two things happen, and through the name of Jesus Christ and the power of the Holy Spirit, can the curse's authority be destroyed.

CHAPTER 13

Demonic Possession

J esus Christ's earthly ministry included preaching the gospel, healing the sick, cleansing lepers, raising the dead, and casting out unclean spirits. In sending out His disciples, Jesus said, "And as you go, preach saying, 'The kingdom of heaven is at hand.' Heal the sick, cleanse the lepers, raise the dead, cast out demons." (Matt. 10:7–8)

Before ascending into heaven, Jesus sent His disciples to preach the gospel to all the nations and promised that signs and wonders would accompany their words:

> "Go into all the world and preach the gospel to every creature. He who believes and is baptized will be saved; but he who does not believe will be condemned. And these signs will follow those who believe: In My name they will cast out demons; they will speak with new tongues; they will take up serpents; and if they drink anything deadly, it will by no means hurt them; they will lay hands on the sick, and they will recover." ...

And they went out and preached everywhere, the Lord working with them and confirming the word through the accompanying signs. (Mark 16:15–18, 20)

The book of Acts speaks of the ministry of the early church:

And believers were increasingly added to the Lord, multitudes of both men and women, so that they brought the sick out into the streets and laid them on beds and couches, that at least the shadow of Peter passing by might fall on some of them. Also a multitude gathered from the surrounding cities to Jerusalem, bringing sick people and those who were tormented by unclean spirits, and they were all healed. (Acts 5:14–16)

And the multitudes with one accord heeded the things spoken by Philip, hearing and seeing the miracles which he did. For unclean spirits, crying with a loud voice, came out of many who were possessed; and many who were paralyzed and lame were healed. (Acts 8:6–7)

Now God worked unusual miracles by the hands of Paul, so that even handkerchiefs or aprons were brought from his body to the sick, and the diseases left them and the evil spirits went out of them. (Acts 19:11–12)

Two thousand years have gone by since the days of the early church, but God hasn't changed. The Devil also hasn't changed, and the people's needs are the same as they were in the past. One of the ministries that Jesus performed in the early church, and one that He commanded us to perform, is to set people free from demonic possession. Those who want to serve people through healing, as Jesus and the apostles did, will no doubt encounter the phenomenon of curses and demonic possession. In the Scripture, we do not find references to anyone doing these types of works before Christ. Were there, however, unclean spirits and demons before Christ? Of course there were.

They provoked Him to jealousy with foreign gods; with abominations they provoked Him to anger. They sacrificed to demons, not to God, to gods they did not know, to new gods, new arrivals that your fathers did not fear. (Deut. 32:16–17)

Rather, that the things which the Gentiles sacrifice they sacrifice to demons and not to God, and I do not want you to have fellowship with demons. (1 Cor. 10:20)

The pagan gods were inhabited by specific demons. Egyptian sorcerers and magicians came against Moses by doing certain miracles through demonic powers.

Sins in the Old Testament that led to the death penalty by stoning led people to demonic possession: idolatry, witchcraft, soliciting spirits, sorcery, fortune-telling, worshipping objects or creation, adultery, incest, homosexuality, bestiality, murder, and open rebellion against one's parents. This isn't even slightly close to being an all-inclusive list of Old Testament sins that were punishable by death.

When God gave the law to Israel, He protected His people from the demonic possession associated with idolatry and all the abominations that occurred during pagan celebrations and indulgences. Unfortunately, because of humankind's disobedience, God's protection was violated. This is why, before the comings of Jesus Christ, some of God's people were afflicted by demons and unclean spirits.

The Devil is skilled in poisoning people while remaining unnoticed. He has managed to deceive many Christians, convincing them that a believer is immune from any type of demonic possession. Can God and a demon really live in one person?

A person's essence is much more complicated than it looks at first glance. When God made Adam from the dust of the earth, and breathed the breath of life into him, humans became living souls (Gen. 2:7). Through disobedience, sin came into humankind.

If we say that we have no sin, we deceive ourselves, and the truth is not in us. (1 John 1:8)

Therefore, just as through one man sin entered the world, and death through sin, and thus death spread to all men, because all sinned. (Rom. 5:12)

When sin entered Adam, another nature was born in him, which the Bible calls the "old man" or the "flesh" (Eph. 4:22; Gal. 5:19; Rom. 6:6). The flesh lives in the body and stands against God and His will:

For to be carnally minded is death, but to be spiritually minded is life and peace. Because the carnal mind is enmity against God; for it is not subject to the law of God, nor indeed can be. (Rom. 8:6–7)

The acts and desires of humankind's sinful nature are known:

Now the works of the flesh are evident, which are: adultery, fornication, uncleanness, lewdness, idolatry, sorcery, hatred, contentions, jealousies, outbursts of wrath, selfish ambitions, dissensions, heresies, envy, murders, drunkenness, revelries, and the like; of which I tell you beforehand, just as I also told you in time past, that those who

135

practice such things will not inherit the kingdom of God. (Gal. 5:19–21)

An unbelieving person has two natures: a soul nature, made by God, and a fleshly nature, which the person received through sin that came down from Adam. When a person receives Jesus into his or her heart, by cross of Jesus his or her flesh is crucified, and yet another nature is birthed in that person. This third nature is God's, and it makes the person a child of God.

But as many as received Him, to them He gave the right to become children of God, to those who believe in His name: who were born, not of blood, nor of the will of the flesh, nor of the will of man, but of God. (John 1:12–13)

The third nature is called the spirit. A life lived in accordance with this nature is called life in the spirit. A continual war is waged between the sinful and the godly nature. The choices made by the soul nature will determine how a person acts in this battle—either in the flesh or by the spirit.

I say then: Walk in the Spirit, and you shall not fulfill the lust of the flesh. For the flesh lusts against the Spirit, and the Spirit against the flesh; and these are contrary to one another, so that you do not do the things that you wish. (Gal. 5:16–17)

A believer therefore has two natures warring within him or her—the spirit and the flesh. Both of these natures have desires, thoughts, and abilities. A believer has eternal life, yet at the same time, death is always present in the person's body. He or she has the ability with one mouth to praise God and to curse people. The person's body can be used either for God or for sin:

> And do not present your members as instruments of unrighteousness to sin, but present yourselves to God as being alive from the dead, and your members as instruments of righteousness to God. (Rom. 6:13)

How can God, who is light, and sin, which is darkness, exist in one person at the same time? How can life and death get along together in one body?

A person has a spirit, soul, and body. When God dwells in a person through the power of the Holy Spirit, He unites the person with his or her spirit and becomes one spirit with that person:

> But he who is joined to the Lord is one spirit with Him. (1 Cor. 6:17)

A person's soul is composed of his or her mind, will, and emotions. The material part of a person is called the body.

A demon or an unclean spirit can live in the body of an individual and control a part of it.

> And He was casting out a demon, and it was mute. So it was, when the demon had gone out, that the mute spoke ... (Luke 11:14)

> Now He was teaching in one of the synagogues on the Sabbath. And behold, there was a woman who had a spirit of infirmity eighteen years, and was bent over and could in no way raise herself up. But when Jesus saw her, He called her to Him and said to her, "Woman, you are loosed from your infirmity." And He laid His hands on her, and immediately she was made straight, and glorified God ... "So ought not this woman, being a daughter of Abraham, whom Satan has bound—think of it—for eighteen years, be loosed from this bond on the Sabbath?" (Luke 13:10–13, 16)

This woman was a daughter of Abraham. She was contorted because Satan had bound her with a spirit of sickness. If this woman had believed in Jesus as her Savior, she would have been saved, but she would have remained contorted until the time that she was delivered from the spirit of illness.

Many unclean spirits are expressed as physical illnesses, and the person affected will not be healed until these spirits are cast out.

Then one was brought to Him who was demon-possessed, blind and mute; and He healed him, so that the blind and mute man both spoke and saw ... Now when the Pharisees heard it they said, "This fellow does not cast out demons except by Beelzebub, the ruler of demons." (Matt. 12:22, 24)

Though this is not always the case, it is not uncommon that behind a chronic or unhealable illness stands an unclean spirit.

Demons and unclean spirits can also control a person's mind and thoughts. A person can hear different voices and can have split personalities. Demons can bring persistent thoughts of murder or suicide, and the spirit of fear can torment a person through various phobias, leading him or her to terror, panic, and emotional paralysis.

The spirit of bondage can also enslave the will of a person. Bondage is most often expressed in harmful habits and lust for a particular sin. Spirits behind addiction, alcoholism, adultery, pornography, lust, television, nicotine, lying, and stealing can enslave a person. These people need to be set free, and unfortunately, a single prayer of repentance and confession is not enough. Those in bondage need the outside help through the prayers of the righteous, who in the name of Jesus release them from captivity.

James says:

> Is anyone among you sick? Let him call for the elders of the church, and let them pray over him, anointing him with oil in the name of the Lord. And the prayer of faith will save the sick, and the Lord will raise him up. And if he has committed sins, he will be forgiven. Confess your trespasses to one another, and pray for one another, that you may be healed. The effective, fervent prayer of a righteous man avails much. (James 5:14–16)

Can people heal themselves through faith? They can. Can they free themselves from the sins that they committed? They can. Can they pray for themselves? Of course, they can. Then why should a person call on someone else, confess his or her sins before that person, and ask that person to pray for him or her? Because God put all of us in one body, and we all need each other. A person's pride always says, I will take care of this myself. I don't need anyone. I will get by without anyone's help. In order to ask for help, we need to have enough humility and courage, and God favors this. He gives grace to those who ask for help.

A person can also be oppresed in emotional ways. This is expressed through the spirit of sadness, depression, self-pity, sorrow, and the like. As was mentioned before, the spirit of rejection often develops from experiencing rejection.

Unclean spirits usually have the same name as the problem that they create. It is possible to be possessed by many spirits, as we see in the biblical example of a man who was grossly possessed by demons that fully owned and controlled him. A whole legion of demons lived in this man, and when they left him, they entered into a herd of two thousand pigs.

Roots of Demonic Strongholds

Demons and unclean spirits are spiritual beings that do not have a physical body. They seek to live in the body of a person or animal so that they may have a home and manifest themselves through that body. Sometimes they come because they were invited, and other times they invade without a reason. When an individual commits a sin leading to death, lives in the flesh, or does not keep him- or herself pure as the Scriptures teach, then that person can be subject to demonic possession. "Be sober, be vigilant; because your adversary the devil walks about like a roaring lion, seeking whom he may devour. Resist him, steadfast in the faith ..." (1 Peter 5:8–9).

This is a rule for Christians so that they can live in freedom and victory, but if a person does not stay alert, that person allows the Devil to invade his or her life. "'Be angry, and do not sin': do not let the sun go down on your wrath: neither give place to the devil" (Eph. 4:26–27).

141

Long-term unforgiveness opens the door to the spirit of unforgiveness, bitterness, and offense.

Witchcraft and all types of occultism lead to demonic possession. If a person is involved in these things, the Devil will surely have a claim on his or her life. If a person abided by old wives' tales, read horoscopes, dabbled in extrasensory activities or fortune-telling, watched horror or satanic films, read magic and occult literature, visited pagan shrines, wore good luck charms, was healed by acupuncture, participated in Eastern martial arts, was carried away by miscellaneous philosophies, listened to satanic music, believed in superstition, or participated in pagan holidays and rituals, then it is possible that he or she might fall under the influence of the power of darkness.

Unclean spirits are also involved in homosexuality, lesbianism, and bestiality. Through suicide and abortion, the spirit of murder and suicide can arise. If a person was raped or was a rapist himself, then the spirit of rape, fornication, or lust may overtake that person. If a person was extremely frightened by something, perhaps in childhood, then he or she may be filled with the spirit of fear. That person will be afraid of the thing that frightened him or her.

Unclean spirits, like sins and curses, can be passed down through inheritance and can control entire families for several generations. The Devil can control a Christian through lying prophecies, various forms of deception, dead religious traditions, force, and manipulation. Unclean spirits are behind all false religions and delusions.

Now the Spirit expressly says that in latter
times some will depart from the faith, giving heed
to deceiving spirits and doctrines of demons ...
(1 Tim. 4:1)

One form of possession is through improper soul at-
tachments.

A young man was in love with a young woman, but for
several reasons, they did not get married, and the man
married another woman. In his heart, he held on to this
first love. He thought about her, dreamed about her, and
indulged in fantasies about her. Even when having inti-
macy with his wife, he imagined that he was with her. He
carried on this way for many years until this soul attachment was finally broken by the power of Jesus's name.

If a person had illicit sex with someone, he or she became one flesh with that person. During the time of the
sexual act, there is also a union on the level of the soul.
Through this physical action a soul attachment is formed,
and the couple leaves each other with a part of him and
herself, a part of their souls. If one of partners had a demonic dependency, then through the soul connection, that
demon might exhort influence on the other partner. The
more sexual connections one has, the more soul connections one will also have. Such a person's heart becomes
fragmented—it cannot belong to one spouse.

The next area of soul ties is related to control and manipulation. There are normal family relationships, having

to do with discipline and child-rearing, and then there are relationships that are dominated by a spirit of control. In such situations, the father or the mother holds the children under such control that even after the children have started their own families, one of the parents continues to exhort control over them. The controller decides where the children will live and what the children will buy and sell. Without the parents' permission, nothing can be done.

Some people have emotional ties to their deceased relatives and don't want to let them go. They mourn for them, miss them, and can't live without them. Others are bound in their souls to the homeland from which they immigrated. They may have already lived in a new country for many years, but all of their thoughts and hearts are in the old country. With the help of God, all of these soul ties need to be broken.

In order for a person's heart to be clean, free, and restored, it is necessary for that person to (if applicable):

1. Repent from sin
2. Forgive all his offenders
3. Receive healing for all spiritual wounds
4. Destroy all curses over his or her life
5. Repent of judging
6. Destroy improper inner decisions
7. Reject negative expectations
8. Break off all improper soul ties
9. Be set free from demonic possession

After doing all of these things, a person will be free to bring to death his or her earthly nature. That person will have dominion over the things of this world, live in freedom, and walk in victory. The Bible says there are many blessings in store for those that fear Him.

One of the greatest benefits is one's baptism and the filling of the Holy Spirit.

CHAPTER 14

Baptism and the Filling of the Holy Spirit

God's Dwelling Place

G od does not wish to be limited to periodic meetings with His children. No matter how sweet, interesting, inspiring, unforgettable, and productive it is, it still comes to an end.

Having created Adam, God came to him in the garden of Eden to have fellowship. We do not know how often these meetings took place, and though Adam was quite happy that God came and went, God was not satisfied. God wanted to have continuous communication with him.

From the moment that Adam ate the forbidden fruit, sin had made a large gap between humankind and God. And while humankind was not concerned by it since it did not understand the fullness of the tragedy that had occurred, God always looked for a way through which the relationship could be restored. For this purpose, sacrifices and ceremonies of purification have been established, and through them, God tried to draw near to humankind.

When Israel walked through the desert to the Promised Land, God commanded Moses to build a tabernacle with a court and an altar so that through the tabernacle and the ceremonies performed in it, God could dwell among Israel.

When David became king, the tabernacle of David was built. It was different from the tabernacle of Moses in the sense that the ark of the covenant was found in a simple tent to which any one person could approach. Animal skins were the only things that separated person from God's glory that found in the tabernacle.

After that, the temple was built. God told Solomon after his prayer about this temple:

> I have heard your prayer and your supplication that you have made before Me; I have consecrated this house which you have built to put My name there forever, and My eyes and My heart will be there perpetually. (1 Kings 9:3)

In the temple, the ark of the covenant was once again hidden in the Holy of Holies.

Of these three places that were intended to be the dwelling place of God and made by human beings, God preferred the tabernacle of David the most, because there God was the closest to His people.

Through the prophet Isaiah, God said, "For thus says the High and Lofty One who inhabits eternity, whose name is Holy: 'I dwell in the high and holy place, with him who has a contrite and humble spirit … '" (Isa. 57:15).

God did not wish to only live in the heavens. He did not wish to live in temples built by human hands. He wished to live in a dwelling place that He made for Himself. From the very beginning, God has chosen Himself a dwelling place in the heart of humankind, but God was unable to do this because in the heart of humankind lived sin. Therefore, one of the reasons behind the coming of Jesus to this earth was to destroy sin. "But now, once at the end of the ages, He has appeared to put away sin by the sacrifice of Himself" (Heb. 9:26).

With the arrival of Jesus Christ, God became even closer to the people. Incarnate God, in the form of Jesus Christ, revealed Himself. He showed His character, love, compassion, and mercy to man. Then God was able to truly be present among the people. He ate, drank, and conversed with them. They were able to touch Him, ask Him questions, and receive answers to their needs; now humankind could see God in human form. Even still, the appearance of God in the body of one man was not enough for God. He wished to settle in and live in every person. The Creator wished to become one with His creation, which He created in His image and likeness. This is made possible through being born again and through humankind's baptism of the Holy Spirit.

A genuine meeting of humankind with the living God brings on repentance, revival, renewal, and liberation. It is the open door to a new relationship between humankind and God, and these relationships are built through the Holy Spirit. God meets with us with the intention of staying with us forever.

Holy Spirit

The Holy Spirit is not just power, anointing, or experience; He is a being and the true God.

In the Old Testament, we see the people on whom the Holy Spirit descended. He descended on the prophets, kings, judges, and priests. Being under the influence of the Holy Spirit, they acquired the ability to do supernatural things.

Samson had a supernatural physical strength. Moses performed miracles and wonders in Egypt and all through the course of the forty years of wandering the wilderness with Israel. The prophet Elijah performed miracles, controlled the heavens, and repeatedly drove fire from the sky. Through his words and actions, the prophet Elisha multiplied oil, blinded an army of enemies, made an ax float, held water, allowed a barren woman to give birth, raised a boy from the dead, healed a leper, and performed many other works of God. All of the prophets in the Old Testament spoke in the name of God, proclaiming God's judgments and the coming of the Messiah to the earth. All of this and so much more was done by the Holy Spirit, who moved through people.

All supernatural things were done when the Spirit of God came upon people and dwelled among them. "Then Samuel took the horn of oil and annointed him in the midst of his brothers; and the Spirit of the Lord came upon David from that day forward …" (1 Sam. 16:13).

When we read about Samson, it is repeatedly said that the Holy Spirit descended on him, but the first person in the Bible who was truly filled with the Holy Spirit was Jesus. "Then Jesus, being filled with the Holy Spirit, returned from the Jordan and was led by the Spirit into the wilderness …" (Luke 4:1).

When Jesus lived on earth in a human body, He represented God, the Father. But everything He did, He did through the Holy Spirit or through the Spirit of God. Through the Holy Spirit, He healed the sick, raised the dead, fed the hungry, cleansed the lepers, cast out demons, and worked various miracles. "How God anointed Jesus of Nazareth with the Holy Spirit and with power, who went about doing good and healing all who were oppressed by the devil, for God was with Him" (Acts 10:38).

Jesus brought Himself as a sacrifice to God through the Holy Spirit: "How much more shall the blood of Christ, who through the eternal Spirit offered Himself without spot to God …" (Heb. 9:14).

In the Old Testament, the Holy Spirit descended upon people, whereas in contrast, Jesus was filled with the Holy Spirit. There's a big difference between the action of the Holy Spirit in these two forms. In the first case, the Holy Spirit came upon a person, and then the person could relay a message or do something through God's power and authority. In the second case, the Holy Spirit dwelled in the person, making Him and the person one whole being. He does not just descend on the person, but is in him or her constantly. "But he who is joined to the Lord is one spirit with Him" (1 Cor. 6:17).

God always had the dream of living inside each person. "I will dwell in them and walk among them. I will be their God, and they shall be My people" (2 Cor. 6:16).

Jesus, being full of the Holy Spirit, became the model for humankind, and after He left us this example, God indwelt in the people. Jesus often referred to Himself as the Son of Man to show us that He is also a true man, just as He is the true God.

The first person who first spoke of the baptism of the Holy Spirit was John the Baptist. When people came to him to be baptized in the Jordan, he said, "I indeed baptize you with water unto repentance, but He who is coming after me is mightier than I, whose sandals I am not worthy to carry. He will baptize you with the Holy Spirit and fire" (Matt. 3:11).

In the last days of His earthly journey, Jesus often spoke with His disciples about the Holy Spirit. He said that it would be better for them when the Holy Spirit came in His place: "Nevertheless I tell you the truth. It is to your advantage that I go away; for if I do not go away, the Helper will not come to you; but if I depart, I will send Him to you" (John 16:7).

Jesus connected His departure with the arrival of the Holy Spirit and also with the fact that those believing in Him would be able to do the same works that He did: "Most assuredly, I say to you, he who believes in Me, the works that I do he will do also; and greater works than these he will do, because I go to My Father" (John 14:12).

Jesus said that the Holy Spirit would dwell in them: "And I will pray the Father, and He will give you another Helper, that He may abide with you forever – the Spirit of truth, whom the world cannot receive, because it neither sees Him nor knows Him; but you know Him, for He dwells with you and will be in you. I will not leave you orphans; I will come to you" (John 14:16–18).

He said that the Holy Spirit would take from Jesus and proclaim to them: "However, when He, the Spirit of truth, has come, He will guide you into all truth; for He will not speak on His own authority, but whatever He hears He will speak; and He will tell you things to come. He will glorify Me, for He will take what is Mine and declare it to you" (John 16:13–14).

After His resurrection, before ascending into the heavens to His father, Jesus told His disciples:

And being assembled together with them, He commanded them not to depart from Jerusalmen, but to wait for the Promise of the Father, "which," He said, "you have heard from Me; for John truly baptized with water, but you shall be baptized with the Holy Spirit not many days from now." ... But you shall receive power when the Holy Spirit has come upon you; and you shall be witnesses to Me in Jerusalem, and in all Judea and Samaria, and to the end of the earth. (Acts 1:4, 8)

The Pentecost

That which John the Baptist spoke about, and that which Jesus promised would happen, occurred on the day of Pentecost. The Holy Spirit, in the form of tongues of fire and loud noise from the heavens, came upon the followers of Jesus Christ, who gathered in the upper room and prayed in expectation for the fulfillment of the promise given by their teacher.

When the Day of Pentecost had fully come, they were all with one accord in one place. And suddenly there came a sound from heaven, as of a rushing mighty wind, and it filled the whole house there they were sitting. Then there appeared to them divided tongues, as of fire, and

153

one sat upon each of them. And they were all filled with the Holy Spirit and began to speak with other tongues, as the Spirit gave them utterance. (Acts 2:1–4)

The day of Pentecost was the beginning of a new era, the era of the Holy Spirit. The descent of the Holy Spirit was proof that Jesus, who was crucified, was resurrected, alive, and is the Lord and Christ.

This Jesus God has raised up, of which we are all witnesses. Therefore being exalted to the right hand of God, and having received from the Father the promise of the Holy Spirit, He poured out this which you now see and hear ... "Therefore let all the house of Israel know assuredly that God has made this Jesus, whom you crucified, both Lord and Christ." (Acts 2:32–33, 36)

When the people of Israel went through the wilderness to the Promised Land, they were with God, who led them with a pillar of cloud by day and a pillar of fire by night. During the day, He protected them from the scorching sun, and by night, he lit the way for them and kept them warm. He led them, nourished them, protected them, and gave them comfort.

That same God that led Israel through the wilderness initially came to this earth in the body of Jesus Christ and after that descended on the day of Pentecost in the form of the Holy Spirit.

Scripture says that over each person that was present in the upper room was a tongue of fire. This means that the same pillar of fire that led the people of Israel through the wilderness now belonged to each individual who was present in that upper room. In the wilderness, there was one pillar of fire for everyone, but now each Christian had within them their own personal pillar. In the wilderness, God was among them, but after that day, He was within them. They were all filled with the Holy Spirit and began to speak in tongues. The Holy Spirit indwelt into each person that was there.

Baptism of the Holy Spirit

Whosoever is born of God can have his own personal loving, kind, and omnipotent God in the form of the Holy Spirit inside him and can have a personal relationship with Him.

This is what God dreamed of from the very beginning. He repeatedly told Israel of the New Testament when He would move into the hearts of people and dwell in them. Before the coming of Christ, the Holy Spirit descended upon the prophets, judges, kings, and priests. In the New Testament, this blessing belongs to all of God's children.

When, on the day of Pentecost, the people saw the apostles and the other Christians with them speaking in different languages and dialects, they marveled and were amazed. The apostle Peter then rose and began to explain this occurrence to them, which is the fulfillment of the prophecy of Joel: "And it shall come to pass in the last days, says God, that I will pour out of My Spirit on all flesh; your sons and your daughters shall prophesy, your young men shall see visions, your old men shall dream dreams. And on My menservants and on My maidservants I will pour out My Spirit in those days; and they shall prophesy ..." (Acts 2:17–18).

After the apostle Peter's sermon, the hearts of the people were touched, and they said, "What shall we do? Then Peter said to them, «Repent, and let every one of you be baptized in the name of Jesus Christ for the remission of sins; and you shall receive the gift of the Holy Spirit. For the promise is to you and to your children, and to all who are afar off, as many as the Lord our God will call" (Acts 2:37–39).

The apostle Peter said that this gift belongs to all those who call upon the Lord. Likewise, the apostle Paul said that this gift belongs to all of God's children: "And because you are sons, God has sent forth the Spirit of His Son into your hearts, crying out, 'Abba, Father!'" (Gal. 4:6).

If salvation through Jesus Christ belongs to the world, then the Holy Spirit belongs to the children of God.

In his sermon on the day of Pentecost, the apostle Peter said that this promise belongs to the Jews, their

156

children, and all those that are far off, whoever the Lord shall call. It belongs to them by promise and by right, but for this promise to be fulfilled, they had to do something: they had to repent and be baptized. As salvation is received through repentance and faith in Jesus Christ, in this same way, the Holy Spirit is obtained through faith and thirst. "This only I want to learn of you: Did you receive the Spirit by the works of the law, or by the hearing of faith?" (Gal. 3:2).

The apostle Paul speaks of guidance in faith; people are capable of believing if they have the knowledge or foundation in God's Word.

Then it is necessary for a person to have a thirst for receiving the Holy Spirit.

> On the last day, that great day of the feast, Jesus stood and cried out, saying, 'If anyone thirsts, let him come to Me an drink. He who believes in Me, as the Scripture has said, out of his heart will flow rivers of living water.' But this He spoke concerning the Spirit, whom those believing in Him would receive; for the Holy Spirit was not yet given, because Jesus was not yet glorified. (John 7:37–39)

The Holy Spirit comes down upon those believers who thirst. Therefore, one must believe and thirst. Jesus also taught that the heavenly Father will give the Holy Spirit to those who will ask Him. "If you then, being evil, know how to give good gifts to your chilren, how much more will your heavenly Father give the Holy Spirit to those who ask Him!" (Luke 11:13).

Here Jesus says that it is necessary to ask the Father for the Holy Spirit, and He will be given to them. When Apostle Paul came to Ephesus, he found certain disciples there. Paul noticed that they lacked something so he asked them:

> Did you receive the Holy Spirit when you be-lieved? So they said to him, "We have not so much as heard whether there is a Holy Spirit." And he said to them, "Into what then were you bap-tized?" So they said, "Into John's baptism." Then Paul said, "John indeed baptized with a baptism of repentance, saying to the people that they should believe on Him who would come after him, that is, on Christ Jesus." When they heard this, they were baptized in the name of the Lord Jesus. And when Paul had laid hands on them, the Holy Spirit came upon them, and they spoke with tongues and prophesied. (Acts 19:2–6)

Christians in Ephesus did not receive the Holy Spirit because they did not know about Him. Because they did not know, they were unable to have faith, and conse-quently, they were unable to thirst for and ask for Him.

Therefore, to be baptized by the Holy Spirit, one must believe in this promise, thirst for its fulfillment, ask God, and receive it.

Repentance, baptism in water, and baptism in the Holy Spirit are three different experiences.

In chapter 8 of the book of Acts, the ministry of Philip in Samaria is described. Through his hands, God performed miracles. Demons were noisily driven out of people, the sick were healed, and there was a great joy in the city. Even a great sorcerer by the name of Simon repented. Everyone, having believed in Christ, got baptized with water.

When the apostles in Jerusalem heard that the Samarians accepted the gospel, they sent apostles Peter and John there to pray for the new believers so they could receive the Holy Spirit. They were all already baptized with water, but the Holy Spirit had not yet descended upon any of them. Apostles Peter and John laid their hands on them, and the Holy Spirit descended upon them. It was so real and apparent that Simon the sorcerer brought the apostles money so that they could give him this kind of authority as well. He wanted whoever he laid his hands on to receive the Holy Spirit too.

Philip taught, healed the sick, and drove out demons, but he did not have the anointing to lay his hands on people to help them receive the Holy Spirit. The Holy Spirit did not descend automatically, not during repentance or during the baptism of water in the name of Jesus. This was done through a completely different experience.

Speaking in Tongues

When the Holy Spirit descends on a person, he receives the supernatural ability to speak in tongues from God. On the day of Pentecost, when the Holy Spirit came down on the disciples and all those who were gathered in the upper room, they all started to speak in tongues. "And they were all filled with the Holy Spirit and began to speak with other tongues, as the Spirit gave them utterance" (Acts 2:4).

When the apostle Peter preached in the home of Cornelius, the Spirit came down on all those gathered there, and they also began to speak in tongues and praise God. "While Peter was still speaking these words, the Holy Spirit fell upon all those who heard the word. And those of the circumcision who believed were astonished, as many as came with Peter, because the gift of the Holy Spirit had been poured out on the Gentiles also. For they heard them speak with tongues and magnify God" (Acts 10:44–46).

During the ministry of Philip in Samaria, there were many who repented and were baptized in water, but not a single person received the Holy Spirit. He did, however, descend on the Samarians in such an apparent way when apostles Peter and John laid their hands on them.

And the multitudes with one accord heeded
the things spoken by Philip, hearing and seeing

the miracles he did ... But when they believed Philip as he preached the things concerning the kingdom of God and the name of Jesus Christ, both men and women were baptized ... Now when the apostles who were at Jerusalem heard that Samaria had received the word of God, they sent Peter and John to them, who, when they had come down, prayed for them that they might receive the Holy Spirit. For as yet He had fallen upon none of them. They had only been baptized in the name of the Lord Jesus. Then they laid hands on them, and they received the Holy Spirit. And when Simon saw that through the laying on of the apostles' hands the Holy Spirit was given, he offered them money ... (Acts 8:6,12,14–18)

During the apostle Paul's time of ministry in Ephesus, the people on which the Holy Spirit came down upon also began to speak in tongues. "When they heard this, they were baptized in the name of the Lord Jesus. And when Paul had laid hands on them, the Holy Spirit came upon them, and they spoke with tongues and prophesied" (Acts 19:5–6).

Therefore, we see that the baptism of the Holy Spirit was not only an inner experience, but it was also accompanied by an external manifestation; people began to speak in other tongues.

"Tongues" is a language of the revived spirit of humankind connected with the Spirit of God. "For he who speaks in a tongue does not speak to men but to God, for no one understands him; however, in the spirit he speaks mysteries ... For if I pray in a tongue, my spirit prays, but my understanding is unfruitful" (1 Cor. 14:2, 14).

When a person prays in tongues, the Holy Spirit intercedes for him or her before God according to the will of God. "Likewise the Spirit also helps in our weaknesses. For we do not know what we should pray for as we ought, but the Spirit Himself makes intercession for us with groanings which cannot be uttered. Now He who searches the hearts and knows that the mind of the Spirit is, because He makes intercession for the saints according to the will of God" (Rom. 8:26–27).

Therefore, the apostles Paul and Jude encourage and urge Christians to pray in spirit or in tongues.

> Praying always with all prayer and supplication in the Spirit, being watchful to this end with all perserverance and supplications for all the saints ... (Eph. 6:18)

> But you, beloved, building yourselves up on your most holy faith, praying in the Holy Spirit, keeping yourselves in love with God ... (Jude 1:20–21)

Prayer in tongues praises God and edifies the person praying.

> He who speaks in a tongue edifies himself ...
> (1 Cor. 14:4)

> Otherwise, if you bless with the spirit ... you indeed give thanks well, but the other is not edified.
> (1 Cor. 14:16–17)

Acts of the Holy Spirit

The Holy Spirit is God Himself in His fullness. Jesus Christ came to reveal and glorify the Father, and the Holy Spirit came to reveal and glorify Jesus Christ. "However, when He, the Spirit of truth, has come, He will guide you into all truth; for He will not speak on His own authority, but whatever He hears He will speak; and He will tell you things to come. He will glorify Me, for He will take of what is Mine and declare it to you" (John 16:13–14).

When Jesus was on the earth, the Holy Spirit lived in His body. After Jesus died, God, the Father, resurrected Him with the power of the Holy Spirit. Through the death and resurrection of Jesus, the Holy Spirit now lives in us, God's children, making us living supernatural organisms and the body of Jesus Christ, which is His church.

And what is the exceeding greatness of His power toward us who believe, according to the working of His might power, which He worked in Christ when He raised Him from the dead and seated Him at His right hand in the heavenly places ... And He put all things under His feet, and gave Him to be head over all things to the church, Which is His body, the fullness of Him who fills all in all. (Eph. 1:19–20, 22–23)

For as the body is one and has many members, but all the members of that one body, being many, are one body, so also is Christ. For by one Spirit we were all baptized into one body—whether Jews or Greeks, whether slaves or free—and have all been made to drink into one Spirit. (1 Cor. 12:12–13)

Living in each person individually, the Holy Spirit creates a temple for God inside us and makes us God's dwelling place.

Having been built on the foundation of the apostles and prophets, Jesus Christ Himself being the chief cornerstone, in whom the whole building, being fitted together, grows into a holy temple in the Lord, in whom you also are being built together for a dwelling place of God in the Spirit. (Eph. 2:20–22)

Work of the Holy Spirit
in the Believer

The first thing that the Holy Spirit does while living in the hearts of believers is complete His work in them. His goal is to change each Christian into the image of Jesus Christ and to grow them into the full measure of His stature. Jesus said that the Holy Spirit will take from Him and transfer it to all believers. "He will glorify Me, for He will take of what is Mine and declare it to you" (John 16:14).

This means that every detail of the sacrifice, death, and resurrection of Jesus is made real for every Christian through the Holy Spirit. The Holy Spirit, through God's Word, changes the way we think, conveys to us and seals in our hearts the feelings of Jesus Christ, and helps us obey God, making the will of God the purpose for our lives.

The Holy Spirit convicts each person in his or her sin and leads that person to repentance. He produces new birth or helps one become born again, and while living in that person, He comforts him or her in affliction, strengthens him or her in sickness, teaches and instructs him or her by God's truth, reveals the future, intercedes for the saints of God according to His will, leads to the knowledge of truth, pours love into the heart of God for His people, inspires hope, produces faith, and gives God's peace.

165

The Holy Spirit is called holy because He represents God's holiness. Only His presence in the life of a person makes this person holy and gives them the desire and ability to live a holy life.

The Work of the Holy Spirit *through* a Believer

The Holy Spirit not only desires to do His work in the heart of everyone but also wants to mightily act through each person. When the Holy Spirit dwells within us, our bodies become His temple and the members of our bodies His instrument.

> Or do you not know that your body is the temple of the Holy Spirit who is in you, whom you have from God, and are you not your own? For you were bought at a price; therefore glorify God in your body and in your spirit, which are God's. (1 Cor. 6:19–20)

> I speak in human terms because of the weakness of your flesh. For just as you presented your members as slaves of uncleanness, and of lawlessness leading to more lawlessness, so now present your members as slaves of righteousness for holiness. (Rom. 6:19)

166

I beseech you therefore, brethren, by the mercies of God, that you present your bodies as a living sacrifice, holy, acceptable to God, which is your reasonable service. (Rom. 12:1)

Jesus promised that every person who believes in Him will be able to do the very things that Jesus did and more. It suddenly became very real when Jesus went to the Father, and through the Holy Spirit, moved into the hearts of His followers.

That which Jesus did while living on this earth in the physical body He is now able to do living through the Holy Spirit in our bodies. Specifically because of this, when leaving the earth to go to the Father, Jesus ordered His disciples not to depart from Jerusalem, but to await the promised Holy Spirit. The Holy Spirit was supposed to give them supernatural power, authority, and anointing. He was supposed to move into them to live through them. The Holy Spirit now lives in us to save people through us, to deliver them, to heal them, to solve their problems, and to fulfill their needs. Sending the disciples out to preach, Jesus promised that God's glory, protection, and authority would accompany them through the power of the Holy Spirit.

And He said to them, "Go into all the world and preach the gospel to every creature.

He who believes and is baptized will be saved; but he who does not believe will be condemned. And these signs will follow those who believe: In My name they will cast out demons they will speak in new tongue; they will take up serpents; and if they drink anything deadly, it will by no means hurt them; they will lay hands on the sick, and they will recover." (Mark 16:15–18)

> Therefore, when the disciples went out and began to do what Jesus told them to, the Holy Spirit reciprocated and began to do what Jesus had promised. "So then, after the Lord had spoken to them, He was received up into heaven, and sat down at the right hand of God. And they went out and preached everywhere, the Lord working with them and confirming the word through the accompanying signs" (Mark 16:19–20).

The Holy Spirit empowers His believers with His gifts and supernatural powers.

> But the manifestation of the Spirit is given to each one for the profit of all: for to one is given the word of wisdom through the Spirit, to another the word of knowledge through the same Spirit, to another faith by the same Spirit, to another gifts of healings by the same Spirit, to another the working of miracles, to another prophecy, to another discerning of spirits, to another different kinds of tongues, to another the

interpretatio of tongues. But one and the same Spirit works all these things, distributing to each one individually as He wills. (1 Cor. 12:7–11)

These gifts were manifested through the apostles during their ministry in Jerusalem.

> And believer were increasingly added to the Lord, multitudes of both men and women, so that they brought the sick out into the streets and laid them on beds and couches, that at least the shadow of Peter passing by might fall on some of them. Also a multitude gathered from the surrounding cities to Jerusalem, bringing sick people and those who tormented by unclean spirits, and they were all healed. (Acts 5:14–16)

This same thing also occurred in Samaria: "Then Philip went down to the city of Samaria and preached Christ to them. And the multitudes with one accord heeded the things spoken by Philip, hearing and seeing the miracles which he did. For unclean spirits, crying with a loud voice, came out of many who were possessed and many who were paralyzed and lame were healed" (Acts 8:5–7).

This also happened in Ephesus and everywhere the Holy Spirit went through the people He lived in. "Now God worked unusual miracles by the hands of Paul, so that even handkerchiefs or aprons were brought from his body to the sick, and the disease left them and the evil spirits went out of them" (Acts 19:11–12).

This became a global movement. "And it happened that the father of Publius lay sick of a fever and dysentery. Paul went in to him and prayed, and he laid his hands on him and healed him. So when this was done, the rest of those on the island who had diseases also came and were healed" (Acts 28:8–9).

The preaching of the gospel must be accompanied by the manifestation of God's power. It was possessed by Christ and His apostles, and if today the Church has the same responsibility of preaching the gospel, then it also is in need of this same power of the Holy Spirit.

Therefore, what must one do to receive the Holy Spirit?

1. Believe that it is necessary;
2. Believe that this gift belongs to all of God's children;
3. Thirst for Him; and
4. Accept Him by faith through the laying of hands or through prayer.

Filling of the Holy Spirit

It is not enough to just accept the Holy Spirit; it is also necessary to be filled with Him. "And do not be drunk with wine, in which is dissipation; but be filled with the Spirit, speaking to one another in psalms and hymns and spiritual songs, singing and making melody in your heart to the Lord ..." (Eph. 5:18–19).

When God baptized humankind with the Holy Spirit, then the Holy Spirit, having moved into us, became connected with our revived spirits and became one Spirit with us. "But he who is joined to the Lord is one spirit with Him" (1 Cor. 6:17).

The Holy Spirit, being in our spirits, no longer leaves, but always dwells in us. Though there are times when we can feel Him, there are other times when we are not able to sense His presence. He became one with us, and therefore, regardless of how we feel, He is always with us and within us. His presence is not dependent on our feelings.

But despite this, our relationship with Him is still dependent on us. If the initiation of the meeting with Adam was God, then now the initiation was handed off from God to man. If in the Old Testament God organized a meeting with humankind, then in the New Testament, humankind has the full right to come before God whenever we may wish.

> Therefore, brethren, having boldness to enter the Holiest by the blood of Jesus, by a new and living way which He consecrated for us, through the veil, that is, His flesh, and having a High Priest over the house of God, let us draw near with a true heart in full assurance of faith, having our

171

> hearts sprinkled from an evil conscience and our
> bodies washed with pure water. (Heb. 10:19–22)

When Jesus lived on the earth, He was always among people, with the exception of when He isolated Himself for prayer. Because of this, everyone who wished could draw near to Him with any need, request, or question. There were times when people got really close to Him in tightly pressing crowds because they wanted to draw near to Him, but not all times of contact resulted in an action from Jesus. If someone touched Jesus to be healed, then the power of God would fall on this person, and they were healed. "And when the men of that place recognized Him, they sent out into all that surrounding region, brought to Him all who were sick, and begged Him that they might only touch the hem of His garment. And as many as touched it were made perfectly well" (Matt. 14:35–36).

One of these people was a woman suffering from a bleeding disorder. She decided in her heart that if she could only touch the hem of Jesus's clothing, she would be healed. During this time, Jesus was in a tightly packed crowd, and many people were touching Him, but only the touch of this woman resulted in a miracle. Everyone else was simply touching the body of a person, but with her faith, she touched God.

This same thing happens through people who are baptized with the Holy Spirit. Some people have the Holy

Spirit inside them, but it reaps them no benefits. Even though He is within them, they are not connected to Him, and they live and act as if He is not with them. Others constantly walk in God's presence and God's power. The Holy Spirit is present in both of these examples of people, but only one of them is filled. Because of this, all Christians have different outcomes.

Therefore, this is why the Word of God calls for us to be filled with the Holy Spirit.

I already spoke of how the Holy Spirit lives in the spirits of people. But besides the spirit, we also have souls and bodies. The soul includes the mind, emotions, and a person's will. The filling of the Holy Spirit is when the Holy Spirit touches the soul of a person and fills it with His presence. People can physically experience the Holy Spirit with their bodies, and the reaction of the body to His presence can be different for each person.

The filling of the Holy Spirit is similar to the filling of the temple with God's glory during Solomon's reign.

> Also King Solomon, and all the congregation of Israel who were assembled with him before the ark, were sacrificing sheep and oxen that could not be counted or numbered for multitude. Then the priests brought in the ark of the covenant of the Lord to its place, into the inner sanctuary of the temple, to the Most Holy Place, under the wings of the cherubim. And it came to pass when

the priests came out of the Most Holy Place (for all the priest who were present had sanctified themselfes, without keeping to their divisions), and the Levites who were the singers, all those of Asaph and Heman and Jeduthun, with their sons and their brethren, stood at the east end of the altar, clothes in white linen, having cymbals, stringed instruments and harps, and with them one hundred and twenty priests sounding with trumpets. And indeed it came to pass, when the trumpeters and singers were as one, to make one sound to be heard in praising and thanking the Lord, and when they lifted up their voice with the trumpets and cymbals and instruments of music, and praised the Lord saying: "For He is good, for His mercy endures forever," that the house, the house of the Lord, was filled with a cloud, so that the priests could not continue ministering be-cause of the cloud; for the glory of the Lord filled the house of God. (2 Chron. 5:6–7, 11–14)

Here we see a picture of when the whole temple was filled with God's glory. It filled the whole temple after all the possessions of the temple were put in proper order, the priests and the Levites were sanctified, countless sac-rifices were brought, and the singers and musicians wholeheartedly praised God. The filling of this temple oc-curred only once.

After this event, God's glory only appeared in the Holy of Holies in a cloud of smoke above the lid of the ark of the covenant. It remained there always, but always intensified when a high priest entered with the blood of animals and incense.

This occurs even today. The Holy Spirit lives in our spirits, but fills all of our beings when we perform certain actions. He could fill all of our souls, or He could just touch a small part. The Holy Spirit can touch our emotions, intellects, and our wills simultaneously, though this does not always occur.

When He touches our emotions, we can experience joy, affection, peace, love, celebration, and so on. All of these experiences have a divine origin, although we experience them through human emotion. Every touch of the Holy Spirit leaves a divine mark on us, and through this, the Holy Spirit conveys to us the feelings of Jesus Christ. The apostle Paul calls them the fruit of the spirit.

"But the fruit of the Spirit is love, joy, peace, longsuffering, kindness, goodness, faithfulness, gentleness, self-control" (Gal. 5:22–23).

Sometime these emotions can go into the body. When filled with the Holy Spirit, a person could cry, sob, tremble, scream, shout, jump, laugh, and so on. All people have different reactions to the presence of God.

When the Holy Spirit touches our minds, we receive supernatural knowledge and revelations. Revelations can be of different orders: revelations of life, revelations of God's will, revelations of God Himself and His ways, and revelations of God's Word.

Through the prophet Isaiah, God said, "For My thoughts are not your thoughts, nor are your ways My ways," Says the Lord. "For as the heavens are higher than the earth, so are My ways higher than your ways, and My thoughts are your thoughts" (Isa. 55:8–9).

Through the filling of the Holy Spirit, God renews our minds. He does not wish for there to be a cosmic distance between His thoughts and ours; He wishes that His thoughts became ours, and when this transition occurs, our lives change.

"And do not be conformed to this world, but be transformed by the renewing of your mind, that you may prove what is that good and acceptable and perfect will of God" (Rom. 12:2).

When the Holy Spirit brings revelation, we can experience inner joy, celebration, and other feelings. Every time this occurs, supernatural faith and hope in God continues to grow and develop in a person.

When the Holy Spirit touches our will, He molds it to match His desires. "For it is God who works in you both to will and to do for His good pleasure" (Phil. 2:13).

After He touches our will, His ways become our ways, and His will becomes the goal of our lives. For Him, we are ready to live, and for Him we are ready to die. Real vision is born in our hearts when the Holy Spirit plants God's desires in us.

Above, I have reviewed the work of the Holy Spirit in us when we are filled with Him. The filling of the Holy Spirit is also necessary so that He can work through us.

By ourselves, we are ordinary people. But when we are filled with the Holy Spirit, we can do that which only God is able to do. When man, having been filled with the Spirit, speaks the Word, it is identical to what God is speaking. Today, we read the message of the apostles and the gospel and accept it as the Word of God because they wrote of their works when they were moved by the Spirit.

On the day of Pentecost, the apostle Peter gained supernatural courage to rebuke the people that had been accomplices in the crucifixion of Jesus Christ. Stephen, standing before the Sanhedrin, the supreme court of Israel, accused those present of having hardened hearts and being rebellious toward God. He stood before them as a representative of God's kingdom, and his face shone like the face of an angel.

When a person, being filled with the Holy Spirit, lays his or her hands on the sick, the sick are healed because in this moment, that person's hands become the hands of Jesus Christ. When that person commands the demons to leave, they flee because behind that person stands the authority and power of God Himself. People can then operate in the gifts of the Holy Spirit that I talked about earlier.

177

The Path to Being Filled
with the Holy Spirit

There are many paths to being filled with the Holy Spirit. The first way is through the speaking of tongues or praying in the spirit:

> For he who speaks in a tongue does not speak to men but to God, for no one understands him; however, in the spirit he speaks mysteries. For if I pray in a tongue, my spirit prays, but my understanding is unfruitful. (1 Cor. 14:2, 14)

When a person prays in tongues, he or she gets filled with the Holy Spirit, and the Holy Spirit intercedes for that person before God according to His will.

"Likewise the Spirit also helps in our weaknesses. For we do not know what we should pray for as we ought, but the Spirit Himself makes intercession for us with groanings which cannot be uttered. Now He who searches the hearts knows what the mind of the Spirit is, because He makes intercession for the saints according to the will of God" (Rom. 8:26–27).

Therefore, the apostles Paul and Jude encouraged and urged Christians to pray in Spirit or in tongues.

"Praying always with all prayer and supplication in the Spirit, and being watchful with all perserverance and supplication for all saints ..." (Eph. 6:18).

"But you, beloved, building yourselves up on your most holy faith, praying in the Holy Spirit, keeping yourselves in the love of God ..." (Jude 1:20–21).

Because the Holy Spirit is connected with the spirit of humankind and lives in us, then we begin to pray with our spirits. The Holy Spirit connects to our prayers and begins to intercede for us. It is during this time that we can be filled with the Spirit.

In the letter to the Ephesians, the apostle Paul opens another path. This is the path of the praise and glorification of God:

"And do not be drunk with wine, in which is dissipation; but be filled with the Spirit, speaking to one another in psalms and hymns and spiritual songs, singing and making melody in your heart to the Lord, giving thanks always for the thing to God the Father in the name of our Lord Jesus Christ" (Eph. 5:18–20).

When we begin to praise and glorify God, all of our attention is focused on Him. During this time, we forget about ourselves, our needs, problems, strengths, and weaknesses. Our whole hearts, minds, feelings, and emotions are directed toward God, and we become maximally vulnerable with God. Then the Holy Spirit, who came to glorify Jesus, is unable to remain indifferent, so He fills us with a holy presence, and we begin to worship God in our spirits.

During this time, we can gaze upon God's glory and be transformed into His image.

"But we all, with unveiled face, beholding as in a mirror the glory of the Lord, are being transformed into the same image from glory to glory, just as by the Spirit of the Lord" (2 Cor. 3:18).

The next path is the prayer of intercession. When a Christian begins to pray in love and compassion for those near and far from him or her, the Holy Spirit helps that Christian because He Himself is the intercessor for the people. He intercedes for people according to the will of God with groanings that cannot be uttered:

"But the Spirit Himself makes intercession for us with groanings which cannot be uttered. Now He who searches the hearts knows what the mind of the Spirit is, because He makes intercession for the saints according to the will of God" (Rom. 8:26–27).

A person can be filled with the Spirit when he or she reads, explores, and ponders over the Word of God. The Holy Spirit came to guide us into all truth, and when we direct our minds to meditate on the Word, the Spirit gives us supernatural revelations for this Word because He Himself is the author of this Word.

The filling of the Holy Spirit also occurs when a Christian preaches or proclaims God's Word. In the book of Acts, an example is given when the apostles Peter, Stephen, and Philip preached while being filled with the Spirit.

People can be filled with the Spirit when they pray for the sick or those afflicted with unclean spirits as well.

I'd like to turn your attention to the fact that the filling of the Holy Spirit can occur through two pathways. Initially, we can be filled with the Spirit, and then, being filled and encouraged, we can begin to preach, praise God, pray, or act through Him. Or the opposite can occur. Initially we can begin to sing, pray, or preach and only then be filled with the Spirit.

In the first case, the Holy Spirit is the initiator of the acts, and a person obeys Him and submits him- or herself to the authority of the Spirit. In the second case, the Holy Spirit inspires and guides a person to do that which he or she is called to in the Word of God, and therefore this Christian just begins to do what is written. The Holy Spirit likes it when people are obedient to the Word of God because by filling us, He gives us the ability to fulfill the will of God.

Thus, an encounter with God brings us to incessant communion with Him through the Holy Spirit, who we need to trust and obey. He gives us revelations of God's Word, changes us into the image of Jesus Christ, anoints us for ministry, and will resurrect us in the last day.

"But if the Spirit of Him who raised Jesus from the dead dwells in you, He who raised up Christ from the dead will also give to your mortal bodies through His Spirit who dwells in you" (Rom. 8:11).

CHAPTER 15

New Position and Revelation of God's Love

After a person is freed from guilt, resentment, emotional wounds, curse, and various addictions, his or her heart is free to be filled with the Holy Spirit and the Word of God. Now the Holy Spirit wishes to reveal the love of God and help that person see him- or herself how God sees that person.

God's Word speaks over and over again about the love of God. No matter how much we read God's Word, however, our minds on their own will not be able to understand this love. Only the Holy Spirit can open to us the depth and fullness of the heavenly Father's unconditional love. This love is higher than our understanding and imagination. Words cannot describe it.

A person's entire life depends on how much he or she understands God's love. Absolutely all Christian virtues, including our salvation, faith, trust, hope, power, patience, and level of sacrifice, are based on this knowledge. A

Christian grows only as much as he or she grows in the knowledge of God's love.

> For this reason I bow my knees to the Father of our Lord Jesus Christ, from whom the whole family in heaven and earth is named, that He would grant you, according to the riches of His glory, to be strengthened with might through His Spirit in the inner man, that Christ may dwell in your hearts through faith; that you, being rooted and grounded in love, may be able to comprehend with all the saints what is the width and length and depth and height—to know the love of Christ which passes knowledge; that you may be filled with all the fullness of God. (Eph. 3:14–19)

Our transformation and fullness in God depends completely on our revelation of God's love. It is precisely this love that attracts us to God, gives us boldness and confidence, and casts from our hearts all fear.

Sometimes people think that God the Father is very strict and far off and that Jesus is so kind, close, and familiar. We feel especially close to Him, but this is because Jesus lived on the earth. Like us, He lived an earthy life, experienced hardships, and suffered terribly, so we think that He is able to empathize with us more. But in fact, the Bible speaks to us about the love of our Father God. It was He who was the initiator of our salvation and redemption.

"For God so loved the world that He gave His only begotten son, that whoever believes in Him shall not perish but have everlasting life" (John 3:16).

The Father God loved us, and therefore He sacrificed the most precious thing He had for the sake of our salvation. The parable of the prodigal son is a proverb about a good and loving father and reveals to us the fatherly heart of God.

After having offended his father, the proud son left his parents' home, and still, the father continued to love him. He was watching for his son's return, and that is why he saw the son approaching when he was still far off. He had waited for that moment for many years and had fully understood how his son's travels would end. His only desire was for his son's return.

Upon seeing his son's familiar, beloved face, the father immediately ran to meet him. His reaction violated all the etiquette and traditions of that time. The father fell on the neck of his son, hugging and kissing him, even though his son was still dirty and smelling of pigs.

The father ordered his servants to bring out his best clothes. The son's belongings were no longer found in the house because he had taken everything when he left, so the father clothed his son in his best clothes from his own wardrobe. He ordered his servants to put his signet ring on the son's hand and to put new shoes on his feet. This testified that the father received him as a true son and inheritor and restored to him all of his rights and privileges.

In honor of his son, the father ordered the servants to slay a fatted calf, play music, and set out a feast (Luke 15).

When a person lives far from God in sin and curse, the heart of the heavenly Father is grieved and sad. God knows the end result of a sinful life, and He paid the ultimate price so that humankind has the opportunity to come back to Him. God sent His beloved Son to earth, so that through the costly torment of Calvary, humankind might be redeemed. He also sent the Holy Spirit, who continually both protects us and reveals our sins, calling us to draw near to the Father.

When a person finally begins to see his or her true condition, the Holy Spirit reveals to that person the crucified Jesus Christ, who then becomes his or her Savior. Through repentance, a person bows his or her heart before the crucified Son of God. There, at the cross, a person's heart, life, and entire being are completely changed.

The heavenly Father removes a person's sinful clothes and clothes him or her in the garments of righteousness. The person becomes righteous just as God is righteous, and God makes him or her an inheritor of all His promises and riches. In that person's honor, God prepares a celebration feast and festivities.

God does not like to rejoice alone. This is spoken of in the entire fifteenth chapter of the book of Luke. This chapter contains three proverbs with the same meaning. In the first, when a shepherd found his missing lamb, he called his friends so that they could rejoice together with him.

In the second, when a woman found a lost piece of silver, she called her friends so that they could share her joy. In the last proverb, when the lost younger son returned, the father asked his older son to share his joy. This is the kind of great joy in heaven over one repentant sinner. The heavenly angels share the joy of the Father God over the return of one of His beloved sons.

When a person comes to God in repentance, God changes his or her name from sinner to righteous one, from cursed to blessed, from fool (if that's what the person has been called) to intelligent, from failure to success, from slave to free person, from rejected to accepted and loved, from foreigner to native, from perishing to saved, and from guilty to justified.

God not only forgives a sinner, but He also justifies him or her. Justification is higher than forgiveness; the guilty one is forgiven, but the justified one is not guilty. A person who is washed in the blood of Christ stands before God as a person who never sinned. God does not know about or remember even one of the forgiven person's past sins. The Father loves this person in the same way that He loves Jesus Christ, and He looks upon this person with pleasure and delight.

Many people who didn't receive adequate love from their fathers as children have a hard time receiving and understanding the unconditional love of God. It is hard for them to believe that God is pleased with them, that He loves them, and that He is delighted with them.

God loves each person because He knit us with His hand in the wombs of our mothers. Before our births, we were in God's heart. As the great designer, He decided what our outward appearances would be; He chose the eyes, ears, noses, hair, mouths, shapes, and other features of our persons. He likes us just as we are.

Every person is unique and matchless. We are the work of the great Master, artist, and Creator. He formed in each of us a unique charm, attractiveness, and set of talents and abilities. Each of our names is written on His palms.

God has an individual relationship with each of His sons and daughters. God doesn't love us collectively; He loves each one of us individually. When He looks at His palms, He doesn't see millions of names, but only one name—yours. He hears only your prayers, He hears only your breathing, and He hears only your songs and your praise. He has this relationship with everyone who is born of Him. Each one of us is very precious and dear to His heart.

Without revelation from the Holy Spirit, we'll never be able to know God and His fatherly love in a real way. Particularly because of this, the apostle Paul pleaded God for the Spirit of revelation for Christians in the church of Ephesus.

"Therefore I also, after I heard of your faith in the Lord Jesus and your love for all the saints, do not cease to give thanks for you, making mention of you in my prayers: that the God of our Lord Jesus Christ, the Father of glory, may give to you the spirit of wisdom and revelation in the knowledge of Him ..." (Eph. 1:15–17).

In the Old Testament, God revealed Himself to the people through the revelation of His various names. He revealed Himself as: God, healer, provider, Omnipotent, shepherd, banner, and other names. Jesus came to reveal God as a loving Father to the people. No one viewed God as the Father before the coming of Christ.

When the disciples of Jesus asked Him to teach them to pray, He gave them the model of prayer that began with the words "Our Father in heaven ..." (Matt. 6:9).

In His prayers and sermons, Jesus constantly called God His Father. He also taught His disciples to call Him Father. In His High Priest prayer, He said, "I have manifested Your name to the men whom You have given Me out of the world ..." (John 17:6).

Jesus was referring to the name Father. John also wrote that to have the first revelation of God means to see Him as a loving Father.

> I write to you, little children, because your sins are forgiven you for His name's sake. I write to you, fathers, because you have known Him who is from the beginning. I write to you, young men, because you have overcome the wicked one. I write to you, little children, because you have know the Father. I have written to you, fathers, because you have known Him who is from the be-

ginning. I have written to you, young men, because you are strong, and the word of God abides
in you, and you have overcome the wicked one.
(1 John 2:12–14)

John speaks of the three phases of spiritual growth that
indicate the level of one's knowledge of God. The very first
thing that a person born from above should know is that
his or her sins are forgiven and that he or she has gained
eternal life. Therefore:

1. Little children know of the forgiveness of their
    sins and know God as their Father.
2. Young people have within themselves the incar-
    nate Word of God and have a practical victory
    over the Devil.
3. Only spiritual fathers know God as the one who
    is from the beginning.

Thus, the very first revelation that has to come through
God's Word and the Holy Spirit is that God is my personal,
loving Father, and I am His beloved son.

Three Levels of Relationships

In Scripture, we find a lot of different kinds of relationships between God and humankind: the Creator and the

189

creation, the Master and the servant, the Vine and the branch, the shepherd and sheep, and many others. I would like to bring your attention to the three different levels of relationships.

When God created Adam from the dust of the earth, they had a relationship on the following level: Creator/creation, God/dust. Disregarding the fact that God created humankind in His image and likeness, though He made us lords over the earth and placed us as masters over the works of His hands, He still called humankind dust. "In the sweat of your face you shall eat bread till you return to the ground, for out of it you were taken; for dust you are, and to dust you shall return" (Gen. 3:19).

While he was in the garden of Eden, there was only one commandment given to the "dust," and it was based on their needs. Adam and Eve only happened to have one single need, and that was the need for food. They did not need absolutely anything else, and to fulfill their one need, God planted the two of them an entire garden. In this garden, there was a tree from which God forbade them to eat.

Adam had a relationship with God right up until he violated God's commandment. As soon as God's decree was broken by humankind, their relationship was destroyed. The loving and kind God declared curse over the land that He created and also punished Adam and Eve. God cast out the "dust" from the garden of Eden that God had created for them, and at the entrance He placed cherubim, who stopped anyone from entering.

Over time, God chose the people of Israel to be His people and built a relationship based on the terms of His law. When His law was obeyed, the relationship was good, and when His law was broken, the relationship was destroyed as well. God expected Israel to follow His commandments; otherwise their lives would be full of curse and destruction.

When the people of Israel obeyed God, everything was good. God protected them, fed them, clothed them, and fulfilled all of their needs. When Israel stepped away from God through idolatry and violation of His commandments, then God would give them into the hands of their enemies, who robbed and oppressed them.

The relationship between God and Israel was equivalent to a lord and his slaves.

> For it is written that Abraham had two sons: the one by a bondwoman, the other by a freewoman ... Which things are symbolic. For these are the two covenants: the one from Mount Sinai which gives birth to bondage, which is Hagar, for this Hagar is Mount Sinai in Arabia, and corresponds to Jerusalem which now is, and is in bondage with her children, but the Jerusalem above is free, which is the mother of us all. (Gal. 4:22–26, emphasis mine)

Israel was at the level of slaves to God. God told the people that the land in which they lived belongs to Him, and if they did not act according to His statutes, then He would cast them out of the land. Unfortunately, that is exactly what happened. Israel was repeatedly led away into captivity and deprived of their land.

But after that, Jesus came! The relationship between God and humankind is now built on completely different conditions.

> But when the fullness of the time had come, God sent forth His Son, born of a woman, born under the law, to redeem those who were under the law, that we might receive the adoption as sons. And because you are sons, God has sent forth the Spirit of His Son into your hearts, crying out, "Abba, Father!" Therefore you are no longer a slave but a son, and if a son, then an heir of God through Christ. (Gal.4:4–7)

God adopted us.

> Blessed be the God and the Father of our Lord Jesus Christ, who has blessed us with every spiritual blessing in the heavenly places in Christ, just as He chose us in Him before the foundation of the world, that we should be holy and without blame before Him in love, having predestined us to adoption as sons by Jesus Christ to Himself, according to thegood pleasure of His will, to the

praise of the glory of His grace, by which He made us accepted in the Beloved. (Eph. 1:3–6)

Through the sacrifice of Jesus Christ, we received new birth.

But many as received Him, to them He have the right to become children of God, to those who believe in His name: who were born, not of blood, nor of the will of the flesh, not of the will od man, but of God. (John 1:12–13)

Through Jesus Christ, we became the children of God. We now have the genetics of our heavenly Father. The apostle John exclaims, "Behold what manner of love the Father has bestowed on us, that we should be called children of God! Beloved, now we are children of God ..." (1 John 3:1–2).

God no longer treats us like dust, nor does he treat us like slaves; we are now His own beloved children. When Adam and Eve sinned, God cast them out of the garden of Eden and out of His sight. When Israel violated God's commandments and didn't fulfill the conditions of the covenant, God cast them out of the Promised Land and deprived them of their blessings and privileges.

But for us, He left His throne and His home in heaven, and in the person of Jesus Christ, came to us on this earth to seek and save us. He understood that we cannot help ourselves, cannot save ourselves, are unable to free ourselves, and are unable to come to Him, so He came to us.

The father from the parable of the prodigal son ran off to meet his son when he was still far off. He left his home to return together with his son. If God cast out Adam, and if He cast out Israel from the Promised Land, then for the sake of His children, He left His home and went to seek and save us. In the person of Jesus Christ, He came to this earth to find the lost humanity.

For our sake, He was beaten, spat upon, humiliated, and rejected. For our sake, He walked to Calvary to pay the penalty for our transgressions. He had to pay with His very own life, and He had to give His blood, spilling it on the cursed cross through the wounds of His pierced hands, feet, and whip-torn body. He had to die on the cross as an infamous criminal with robbers, face death, and come face-to-face with the Devil.

He had to take upon Himself all of our sins, crimes, vices, and lawlessness. Through blows from the whips and sticks, He took all of our sickness and disease. Through the crown of thorns that was laid upon His holy head, He took all of our curses. He had to drink the bitterness of vinegar and bile.

- ❏ He became sin so that we could be righteous.
- ❏ He was cursed so that we may be blessed.
- ❏ He was wounded so that we could be healed.
- ❏ He was rejected so that we could be accepted.

194

- ❑ He was slandered so that we could be justified.
- ❑ He was humiliated so that we could be lifted up.
- ❑ He was disgraced so that we could be glorified.
- ❑ He thirsted so that we could be filled.
- ❑ He became poor so that we could be rich.
- ❑ He was lonely so that we could be in a big family.
- ❑ He was stripped so that we could put on the garments of glory.
- ❑ He had a crown of thorns so that we could wear the crown of life.
- ❑ He died so that we could have eternal life.

Our heavenly Father never casts out those who come to Him. The door to His home and kingdom is always open to His children. Through the blood of Jesus Christ, we can always come into His presence to the throne of grace and mercy.

If God gave His Son for the sake of sinners, how can He not also freely give us all things? He wished that we could come to know Him as a kind, gentle, generous, and loving Father.

Expression of God the Father through His Son, Jesus

To be able to see the love of God the Father, all you have to do is look at His Son, Jesus. Jesus came to this earth to reveal and show the heavenly Father. One day, His disciple, Philip, asked Jesus:

> "Lord, show us the Father, and it is sufficient for us." Jesus said to him: "Have I been with you so long, and yet you have not known Me, Philip? He who has seen Me has seen the Father; so how can you say, 'Show us the Father'? Do you not believe that I am in the Father, and the Father in Me? The words that I speak to you I do not speak on My own authority; but the Father who dwells in Me does works. Believe Me that I am in the Father and the Father in Me ...'" (John 14:8–11)

This is the Father, in the form of Jesus Christ, who walked upon this earth. It was He who stretched out His hands to the lost sheep of the house of Israel. It was He who healed the sick, fed the hungry, cleansed the lepers, resurrected the dead, and comforted the mourning. It was He who forgave the woman caught in adultery. It was He that went to the tax collectors and the sinners and ate in their company. It was He who called to the people: "Come to Me, all you who labor and are heavy laden, and I will give you rest" (Matt. 11:28).

This is the Father that leaves the ninety-nine sheep and goes to look for that one single lost sheep. It was He who washed the feet of His disciples, and it was He who sacrificed His soul for us. He agreed to share with us our destiny so that we might have His glory. He proved His love for us when we were still sinners. "But God demonstrates His own love toward us, in that while we were still sinners, Christ died for us" (Rom. 5:8).

God the Father cannot be seen while in the body, so He sent His Son so that Jesus could show through Himself the love and character of the Father.

> No one has seen God at any time. The only begotten Son, who is in the bosom of the Father, He has declared Him. (John 1:18)

God wishes that we would be rooted and grounded in His love, which elevates human intelligence and understanding. Just like mercy, it is higher than the heavens. "For your mercy is great above the heavens ..." (Ps. 108:4).

Every Christian must receive the revelation of God's love and that he or she is a child of God. Every Christian must understand that he or she is not just a child of God, but also His dearly beloved. Unfortunately, not many can say a lot about their relationships with God. Many Christians are found in the church as if they're in an orphanage. They don't know what it means to be loved, and even more so, what it means to be tenderly loved. It's not because God doesn't love them, but because they are not familiar with His love.

These people are similar to the eldest son from the parable of the prodigal son; they constantly try to earn something from God. They cannot believe that everything that belongs to their Father belongs to them as well. Their lives fall into spiritual poverty, sorrow, discontentment, and grumbling. The father said, "Son, you are always with me, and all that I have is yours" (Luke 15:31).

The reason for this mentality is found in the fact that the eldest son was too busy with the ministry that he lacked the time to build a relationship with his father, so he did not know him.

Today, the heavenly Father, like before, is looking for His busy sons and daughters to caress, comfort, heal, please, and share with them a celebratory dinner. Even today, He stands at the doors of our hearts and knocks, and if someone hears His knock and opens the door, He will happily come in and share the evening with him.

The roots of faith in every Christian should grow in the depths of God's love. The apostle Paul was rooted in it so much that he boldly said,

> Who shall separate us from the love of Christ? Shall tribulation, or distress, or persecution, or famine, or nakedness, or peril, or sword? ... For I am persuaded that neither death nor life, nor angels nor principatlities nor powers, nor things present nor things to come, not height nor depth, nor any other created thing, shall be able to separate us from the love of God which is in Christ Jesus our Lord. (Rom. 8:35, 38–39)

Rootedness or confidence in God's love helps a person go through all the difficulties, hurricanes, and storms of life. Confidence in God's love is the platform for a life without worries, fears, and negative experiences. God's love is a safe harbor, a strong rock, and the stable and mighty hand of God. It is a tender Father's heart.

Main Foundation of Confidence in the Fact That You're Loved

Where does one get the confidence that God doesn't love just all His children, but loves each one specifically? What should my faith be based on in regard to God's love for me?

Once, Israel asked God, "In what way have You loved us?" (Mal. 1:2)

God told the people of Israel that He loves them, and they began to argue with Him, wishing that He would have brought them good evidence for His claim. Of course, God could give them a lot of evidence on the basis of what He has done for them. He could list all the care that He showed them. He could remind them of all the miracles that He did for them and their sake, but He did mention any of this.

He said that He loved Israel, but detested Esau, although they were brothers born on the same day. God wanted to show that His love for Israel has been revealed

199

through making them His chosen ones. God chose Israel and showed them His mercy through showing His concern in their endeavors, His protection, His help, and through the many miracles He worked for their sakes.

If Queen Esther asked the King Ahasuerus if he can prove that he loves her, then he could bring to her a lot of convincing evidence. He could tell her that because of him, she lives in a royal palace, eats royal cuisine, sits on the royal throne, and has the royal crown. But the most important evidence was that out of thousands of beautiful girls, he chose her. This is why she has all the royal privileges and honors.

The most important proof that God loves me is that among six billion people that are no worse than me, God chose me. The fact that I am a Christian is not a matter of chance. I did not accidentally end up in church or at an evangelism, and I was not accidentally born into a family of believers. God chose me, and because of this, I was born into this world. God has no accidental or unwanted children; all of His children are welcome and loved. Therefore, because of these events, I was able to hear about God, repent, and be saved. "Of His own will He brough us forth by the word of truth, that we might be a kind of first-fruits of His creatures" (James 1:18).

And now, because I am His son, He shows for me His fatherly care. All the good that I have today is the result of me being His son. And I am His son because He wanted me to be born; I was chosen before the foundation of the world.

"Blessed be the God and Father of our Lord Jesus Christ, who has blessed us with every spiritual blessing in the heavenly places in Christ, just as He chose us in Him before the foundation of the world, that we should be holy and without blame before Him in love, having predestined us to adoption as sons by Jesus Christ to Himself ..." (Eph. 1:3–5).

Since God chose me, He has a plan for my life. My destiny is in His hands, and from them, no one will snatch me. He will never leave me nor forsake me. He is always with me, for me, and within me.

Jesus came to this earth for my sake. He took my place, so all the riches of His sacrifice could be mine. Whenever Jesus used the word believer, He was referring to me.

Therefore, it does not matter what is happening around me, what circumstances I live in, and how much I have or do not have. It does not matter if I get the answers to my questions or requests, whether I'm sick or healthy, whether I'm well-off materially or not—none of this plays a role in whether I am confident in God's love. All external circumstances and experiences such sorrow and suffering, joy and gladness, success and abundance are not the main indicators of God's love for me.

Only a person perfectly confident in God's love for him or her can believe that: "We all know that all things work together for good to those who love God, to those who are the called according to His purpose" (Rom. 8:28).

A person with faith in the love of God is deeply rooted in the Word of God and the sacrifice of Jesus Christ. Such a person will never offend of God.

What God's Love Did for Me

The apostle Paul writes in great detail in his letters to the Romans and others about who he was before his revival.

I had the following traits:

1. By nature, I was a sinner.
2. Because I was a sinner, I sinned continuously.
3. Sin had power over me.
4. The law of sin and death was working within me, and I was under its authority.
5. The sinful nature of Adam, that opposed God, lived inside me.
6. I was under the law, which demanded from me something that was beyond my strength.
7. Law caused the existence of sin, so it seduced me and produced in me desires, and I sinned.
8. Due to the fact that I sinned, the Devil constantly convicted me before God.
9. I lived with feelings of guilt.
10. I was under God's wrath and condemnation, even though He loved me very much.

11. I was spiritually dead and lived by the way of the world and the will of the Devil.
12. I was in opposition with God.
13. Death, eternal damnation, and hell were awaiting me.

For God so loved the world that He gave His only begotten Son, that whoever believes in Him should not perish but have everlasting life. (John 3:16).

Jesus came to save His people from their sins. He was deprived of His power and exposed to shame, but He destroyed all the works of the Devil. In His death and resurrection, He conquered death and hell and released all the prisoners to freedom.

My Benefits in the Sacrifice of Jesus Christ

1. Jesus took away my sin.
2. Jesus paid for all my sin.
3. Jesus saved me from God's judgment and wrath.
4. Jesus revived me.
5. Jesus gave me a new heart and a new life.
6. Jesus made me an entirely new creation.

7. Jesus reconciled me with God.
8. Jesus made me God's son and heir.
9. Jesus freed me from the power of sin.
10. Jesus freed me from the law.
11. Jesus freed me from all curse.
12. Jesus healed me from all sickness and disease.
13. Jesus led me into His kingdom.
14. Jesus filled me with His Spirit.
15. Jesus made me the righteousness of God.
16. Jesus poured His love into my heart.
17. Jesus settled in me all His greatness and might.
18. Jesus became one Spirit with me.
19. Jesus implanted me into His body.
20. Jesus gave me eternal life.
21. Jesus created for me an opening into God's presence.
22. Jesus gave me authority over the forces of the darkness.
23. Jesus gave me authority to cast out demons and heal people.
24. Jesus gave me an eternal inheritance.
25. Jesus made me complete.
26. Jesus put me in Him in heaven.

When I came to God in repentance, He revived me and placed me in Jesus Christ. Since then, I am found in Him, and absolutely everything that I have, I have only in Him.

I Am in Him

1. I am chosen by God before the creation of the world.

    Just as He chose us in Him before the foundation of the world ... (Eph. 1:4)

2. God foreknew me.

    For whom He foreknew ... (Rom. 8:29)

3. He organized for me to be transformed into the image of His Son, Jesus Christ.

    He also predestined to be conformed to the image of His Son ... (Rom. 8:29)

4. I am called, justified, and glorified.

    Moreover whom He predestined, these He also called; whom He called, these He also justified; and whom He justified, these He also glorified. (Rom. 8:30)

5. I am born of God and am therefore God's son and heir.

Therefore you are no longer a slave but a son, and if a son, then an heir of God through Christ. (Gal. 4:7)

6. I'm saved and sanctified.

For by grace you have been saved through faith, and that not of yourselves; it is the gift of God ... (Eph. 2:8)

By that we have been sanctified through the offering of the body of Jesus Christ once from all. (Heb. 10:10)

7. I am the righteousness of God.

For He made Him who knew no sin to be sin for us, that we might become the righteousness of God in Him. (2 Cor. 5:21)

8. I am connected with Christ. He is in me, and I in Him.

Do you not know yourselves, that Jesus Christ is in you? (2 Cor. 13:5)

But of Him you are in Christ Jesus ... (1 Cor. 1:30)

Which is Christ in you, the hope of glory. (Col. 1:27)

9. I am a new creation.

Therefore, if anyone is in Christ, he is a new creation. (2 Cor. 5:17)

10. I am a participant in the heavenly calling.

Therefore, holy brethren, partakers of the heavenly calling ... (Heb. 3:1)

11. I am a son of the kingdom.

The good seeds are the sons of the kingdom. (Matt. 13:38)

12. I have eternal life.

He who has the Son has life ... (1 John 5:12)

13. I was chosen to be rich in faith, and an heir of the kingdom.

Has God not chosen the poor of this world to be rich in faith ad heirs of the kingdom ... (James 2:5)

14. I am God's property.

    You are not your own ... for you were bought at a price. (1 Cor. 6:19)

15. My life is hidden with Christ in God.

    For you died, and your life is hidden with Christ in God. (Col. 3:3)

16. It is no longer I who live, but Christ who lives in me.

    It is no longer I who live, but Christ lives in me; and the life which I now live in the flesh I live by faith in the Son of God ... (Gal. 2:20)

17. My body is the temple of the Holy Spirit and the members of Jesus Christ.

    Do you not know that your bodies are the members of Christ? Or do you not know that your body is the temple of the Holy Spirit who is in you ... (1 Cor. 6:15, 19)

18. Sin has no power over me.

    We died to sin. (Rom. 6:2)

19. The Devil can not blame me because God justifies me, and Jesus intercedes for me.

Who shall bring a charge against God's elect? It is God who justifies. Who is he who condemns? It is Christ who dies, and furthermore is also risen, who is even at the right hand of God, who also makes intercession for us. (Rom. 8:33–34)

20. I am free from all sickness and disease.

Surely He was borned our griefs and carried our sorrows ... And by His stripes we are healed. (Isa. 53:4–5)

21. I am redeemed from the empty way of life handed to me from my forefathers.

You are not redeemed with corruptible things, like silver or gold, from your aimless conduct received by tradition from your fathers ... (1 Peter 1:18)

22. I have the fullness of God.

For in Him dwells all the fullness of the Godhead bodily; and you are complete in Him, who is the head of all principality and power. (Col. 2:9–10)

23. I am forever complete.

For by one offering He has perfected forever those who are being sanctified. (Heb. 10:14)

24. I am a partaker of God's nature.

That through these you may be partakers of the divine nature ... (2 Peter 1:4)

25. On me rests the Spirit of glory.

Blessed are you, for the Spirit of glory and of God rests upon you. (1 Peter 4:14)

26. I am filled with the Holy Spirit.

For by one Spirit we were all baptized into one body ... and have all been made to drink into one Spirit. (1 Cor. 12:13)

27. I am engaged to Jesus Christ.

For I have betrothed you to one husband, that I may present you to Christ. (2 Cor. 11:2)

28. I have power over all the forces of darkness.

Behold, I give you the authority to trample on serpents and scorpions, and over all the power of the enemy, and nothing shall by any means hurt you. (Luke 10:19)

29. I am more than a conqueror.

Now thanks be to God who always leads us in triumph in Christ, and through us diffuses the fragnance of His knowledge in every place. (2 Cor. 2:14)

30. I am seated in heaven.

And raised us up together, and made us sit together in the heavenly places in Christ Jesus ... (Eph. 2:6)

31. I have the power to heal the sick and cast out demons.

And these signs will follow those who believe: In My name they will cast out demons ...
They will lay hands on the sick, and they will recover. (Mark 16:17–18)

32. I am a king and a priest of God.

And have redeemed us to God by Your blood out of every tribe and tongue and people and nation, and have made us kings and priests to our God ... (Rev. 5:10)

33. Everything I say with faith will be.

For assuredly, I say to you, whoever says to this mountain, 'Be removed and be cast into the sea,' and does not doubt in his heart, but belives that those things he says will be done, he will have whatever he says. (Mark 11:23)

34. God loves me like He loves Jesus.

You have sent Me, and have loved them as You have loved Me. (John 17:23)

35. I can do the works that Jesus did, and even more.

Most assuredly, I say to you, he who believes in Me, the works that I do he will do also; and greater works than these he will do, because I go to My Father. (John 14:12).

36. I am not of this world, but of God.

You are not of the world, but I chose you out of the world ... (John 15:19)

You are of God, little children, and have over-come them, because He who is in you is greater than he who is in the world. (John 4:6).

37. I am a person of God.

   But you, O man of God ... (1 Tim. 6:11)

38. I am the image and glory of God.

   Since he is the image and glory of God ...
(1 Cor. 11:7)

39. I am blessed with every spiritual blessing in the
   heavens.

   Blessed be the God and Father of our Lord
Jesus Christ, who has blessed us with every spir-
itual blessing in the heavenly places in Christ.
(Eph. 1:3)

40. I have access to the Father.

   For through Him we both have access by one
Spirit to the Father. (Eph. 2:18)

41. I have access to grace.

   Through whom also we have access by faith
into this grace in which we stand, and rejoice in
hope of the glory of God. (Rom. 5:2)

42. I am the light of the world and salt of the earth.

You are the salt of the earth ... You are the light of the world. (Matt. 5:13–14)

43. I am God's coworker.

For we are God's fellow workers. (1 Cor. 3:9)

44. I am Christ's fragrance.

For we are to God the fragrance of Christ ... (2 Cor. 2:15)

45. I'm in covenant with God.

This cup is the new covenant in My blood. (1 Cor. 11:25)

46. I will never hunger or thirst.

I am the bread of life. He who comes to Me shall never hunger, and he who believes in Me shall never thirst. (John 6:35)

47. Coming to God, I will never be cast out.

And the one who comes to Me I will by no means cast out. (John 6:37)

48. I have life with abundance.

I have come that they may have life, and that they may have it more abundantly. (John 10:10)

49. I will receive anything that I ask in the name of Jesus Christ.

Therefore I say to you, whatever things you ask when you pray, believe that you receive them, and you will have them. (Mark 11:24)

And whatever you ask in My name, that I will so, that the Father may be glorified in the Son. (John 14:13)

50. I have everything pertaining to life and godliness.

As His divine power has given to us all things that pertain to life and godliness … (2 Peter 1:3)

51. I have an anointing from the Holy One and know everything.

But you have an anointing from the Holy One, and you know all things. (1 John 2:20)

215

52. I am sent by Jesus, just as Jesus was sent by the Father.

   As the Father has sent Me, I also send you. (John 20:21)

53. My residence is in heaven.

   For our citizenship is in heaven ... (Phil. 3:20)

54. I will judge the world and the angels.

   Do you not know that the saints will judge the world? (1 Cor. 6:2)

   Do you not know that we shall judge the angels? (1 Cor. 6:3)

55. I will reign with Christ forever and ever.

   And they shall reign forever and ever. (Rev. 22:5)

All of this happened because of God's love and the sacrifice of Jesus Christ. When people clearly understands who they were before, what they had and what awaited them, and also see what they have become and what they now have, their hearts fill with tremendous delight, deep gratitude, and unspeakable joy. Through this understanding, people develop a responsive love for God, a desire to live for Him, and a desire to serve Him wholeheartedly. A person in such a state is able to love someone who, like him or her, is born of God.

In His Word, as in the letters, our heavenly Father left us sweet words that express His love, loyalty, devotion, and care. This letter is addressed to you and everyone who is born of God.

A Letter from the Loving Father

My dear child! How little you know of Me, but I know everything about you. I know when you sit down and when you stand up. I know all your thoughts and ways. Before a word is even on your tongue, I already know what you will say. Even the hairs of your head are numbered by Me.

I created you in My image and in My likeness. You live in Me and have your being in Me. You are from My royal family. Before I even formed you in the womb of your mother, I knew you. I choose you before the foundation of the world. You are not an accident. In My book are written all the days that are meant for you. It was I who determined the time of your birth and the limits of your habitation.

My wonderful child, I carefully wove you in the womb of your mother, and on the day of your birth, I called you out. I have been with you all of your days, and with great love, I have waited for you to turn to Me. I stood at the door of your heart and knocked.

Here I am beside you, and there is no evil in Me. I am full of love for you and yearn to give it all to you. This is because you are My child, and I am your Father. I want to give you more than your earthly father can give because I am the perfect Father. I love you unconditionally and eternally and know all that you need.

My thoughts toward you, like the sand of the seashore, cannot be numbered. I rejoice over you in My heart and am tirelessly working well for you. You are my riches; that's why I will strengthen you. I will show you great and incomprehensible things that you have yet to know. If only you knew how much good I have that I am saving for you. I can do incomparably more for you than you can ask or even think.

Comfort yourself in Me, and I will fulfill the desires of your heart. I am a merciful Father and the God of all comfort. I hear when you call upon Me. As a loving Father, I will take you in My arms, and I will carry you to My breast. No one can take you from My arms and cause you evil.

I love you as I love My Son, Jesus. For your sake I gave Him over to desecration, torment, and death. In Him I revealed My love for you. In Him I was reconciled with you. I am not against you; I am for you. No one and nothing can separate you from My love in Jesus Christ.

There is coming a day when I will wipe away all tears from your eyes and remove all pain that you have had to experience on this earth. And when you come to My eternal home in heaven, I will have an unprecedented feast for you that will never end. Seek Me with all of your heart. I am waiting for you and your reciprocal love.

Your loving heavenly Father.
(Rephrased from the Bible text)

CHAPTER 16

Physical Healing: Redemption Includes Healing

After we were delivered from guilt, resentment, and unforgiveness, we received inner healing and were freed from curse and from demonic bondage; when our hearts are filled with the Holy Spirit and God's love, it's easy for us to receive physical healing. On the cross of Calvary, Jesus paid not only for our sins, but also for our sickness and disease.

> Surely He has borne our griefs and carried our sorrows ... But He was wounded for our transgressions, He was bruised for our iniquities; the chastisement for our peace was upon Him, and by His stripes we are healed, (Isa. 53:4–5)

> He Himself took our infirmities and bore our sickness. (Matt. 8:17)

> Who Himself bore our sins in His own body on
> the tree, that we, having died to sins, might live
> for righteousness—by whose stripes you were
> healed. (1 Peter 2:24)

Redemption includes not only the forgiveness of sins and deliverance from all spiritual captivity, but also physical healing. Sickness and disease came into the world because of Adam's sin. Jesus came into this world to fulfill the law and died on the cross to redeem and deliver us not only from sin, but from its effects, one of which is disease.

God has many different names, which are determined by His nature and character. During Israel's exit from the land of Egypt, He revealed Himself to them as God the healer.

"If you diligently heed the voice of the Lord your God and do what is right in His sight, give ear to His commandments and keep all His statues, I will out none of the diseases on you which I have brought on the Egyptians. For I am the Lord who heals you" (Ex. 15:26).

God not only spoke of the fact that He is a healer, but He completed the full healing of the entire nation in one night when he was leading them out. "He also brought them out with silver and gold, and there was none feeble among His tribes" (Ps. 105:37).

On the last night before their exodus, Israelites had to slaughter a lamb, anoint the doorposts of their house with its blood, roast the lamb over a fire, and eat unleavened bread and bitter herbs with their whole family.

The sacrifice of the Passover lamb was made not only for the deliverance of the Jewish firstborn from death, but it also healed all the sick among their nation. The blood of the lamb on the doorposts protected the firstborns from the angel of death, and the body of the lamb, which they had to eat by morning, brought all of the participants of the meal full healing from all forms of diseases.

Over the hundreds of years of slavery in Egypt, the people became poor and crippled from the whips and sticks of the Egyptians. They developed a variety of diseases and infirmities, and in this state, they were unable to make the long journey through the desert. Because of this, God used the Passover lamb's death to bring them salvation and their bodies healing. The Passover lamb became the model for the sacrifice of Jesus Christ, which was given for our salvation.

King David knew God as a healer. This is why he commanded his soul:

> Bless the Lord, O my soul; And all that is within me, bless His holy name! Bless the Lord, O my soul, and forget not all His benefits: Who forgives all your iniquities, who heals all your diseases, Who redeems your life from destruction, Who crowns you with loving kindness and tender mercies, Who satisfies your mouth with good

things, so that your youth is renewed like the eagle's. (Ps. 103:1–5)

Jesus walked in the complete will of His Father and opened His Father's heart, will, and desires to the people. All that He saw in the Father, he replicated on earth, and all that He heard from the Father is what He spoke.

Healing for Everyone

When carefully examining the Scriptures, we do not find a single instance where Jesus refused anyone healing.

> When evening had come, they brought to Him many who were demon-possessed. And He cast out the spirits with a word, and healed all who were sick. (Matt. 8:16, emphasis mine)

> Then Jesus went about all the cities and villages, teaching in their synagogues, preaching the gospel of the kingdom, and healing every sickness and every disease among the people. (Matt. 9:35, emphasis mine)

> And great multitues followed Him, and He healed them all. (Matt. 12:15, emphasis mine)

And when Jesus went out He saw a great multitude; and He was moved with compassion for them, and healed their sick. (Matt. 14:14)

And when the men of that place recognized Him, they sent out into all the surrounding region, brought to Him all who were sick, and begged Him that they might only touch the hem of His garment. And as many as touched it were made perfectly well. (Matt. 14:35–36)

Then great multitudes came to Him, having with them the lame, blind, mute, maimed, and many others; and they laid them down at Jesus; feet, and He healed them. (Matt. 15:30)

Then the blind and the lame came to Him in the temple, and He healed them. (Matt. 21:14)

Other than these mass healings, we also see many individual healings, and not a single time did Jesus refuse anyone healing. Even a Canaanite woman who had absolutely no right to be healed was heard, and her suffering daughter was healed and delivered demons.

Jesus showed God's attitude toward disease by healing without exception. When sending His disciples to preach the gospel, Jesus commanded them to heal the sick everywhere and always.

And when He had called His twelve disciple to Him, He gave them power over unclean spirits, to cast them out, and to heal all kinds of sickness and all kinds of disease. These twelve Jesus sent out and commanded them, saying: And as you go, preach, saying, "The kingdom of heaven is at hand." Heal the sick, cleanse the lepers, raise the dead, cast out demons. Freely you have received, freely give. (Matt. 10:1, 5, 7–8, emphasis mine)

God Wishes to Heal

Once, a leper came to Jesus: "And behold, a leper came and worshiped Him, saying, 'Lord, if You are willing, You can make me clean.' Then Jesus put out His hand and touched him, saying, 'I am willing; be cleansed.' Immediately his leprosy was cleansed" (Matt. 8:2–3).

In the form of a leper, we are able to see all the sick people of the world. To the question: "Lord, do you wish it?" There is only one answer: "I do wish." What did the leper do? He allowed Jesus to make His wish a reality.

"Jesus, You wish to heal, so complete this on me."

Many people believe that God is all powerful, and can heal, but they find it difficult to believe that it is them that He wishes to heal and right in that exact moment. So they pray: "O Lord! If it is Your will, then heal me."

God not only has the ability to heal, but He also showed that He wants to heal everyone through Jesus Christ. God wants to heal each person as strongly as He wishes to save each person.

If I had the opportunity to save a person from death, but did not take this opportunity or didn't want to, then even with the law of justice, I would have been convicted. We have already spoken of how salvation includes healing; God especially wishes for all people to be saved and to come to the knowledge of truth.

God wants His children to be healthy more than His children wish themselves to be healthy. This is why Jesus took all of our infirmities and bore our diseases. Jesus withstood thirty-nine lashes from a whip, and it is not coincidental that medicine states that there are thirty-nine different categories of disease. Jesus took all that disease into His body in a physical, practical, and real way so that His children could be healthy.

Why was God interested in the healthy bodies of His children? Firstly, because He is full of love and compassion. God allows suffering in the lives of His children when He is able to find some kind of use from it, but He is not interested in seeing His children suffer without any necessity. Secondly, God wants healthy workers on His field that will be able to go to the ends of the earth and bring the gospel with them. Thirdly, God wishes that all the things for which He paid for with a high price on the cross become the property of his children.

Healing—this is the food that belongs to God's children. Jesus once answered this way to a pagan woman who was asking Him for the healing of her daughter. "Let the children be filled first, for it is not good to take the children's bread and throw it to the little dogs" (Mark 7:27).

Here it speaks of healing and deliverance as the bread of the children, and it belongs to His children. There is not one instance in God's Word where a person came to Jesus for healing, and He denied it to him.

Therefore, God can heal each person, and He wants this to happen very much.

The Healing Is
Already Complete

The redemption of people has already been done, and the price has already been paid. Jesus already carried the sins and diseases of the people and already took upon Himself our infirmities. Therefore there is no longer any need to carry them because by His wounds, we are already healed.

Many people, in spite of their doubts in regards to the will of God, earnestly try to rid themselves of their illnesses and everything that torments them. They look for the best doctors, spend money on medications, read books, and use traditional medicines just to become healthy. In this way, they seem to say: "Lord, I do not know what You want, but I want to be healthy and will do everything possible from my side." Instead of finding the will of God and using the benefits of the grace of God, they go in circles, looking for help in medicines and doctors. Is it not better to stand with God in faith against their diseases? Because it is a lot more effective.

A woman suffering of a bleeding disorder for many years, after spending all her money on doctors, finally realized that her only way out was through Jesus. Initially, she acted upon the principle: "You can do as You wish, God, but I want to be healthy, so I will pay any money for my health." She spent everything, tried everything, lost time, and progressed to an even worse condition. She was finally convinced that this was not the formula or the solution to her problems.

She then decided to use a different option. She had heard of Jesus, and perhaps even saw people who were delivered and healed by Him, so she thought to herself: I know that He heals everyone with His Word or by touching them. He never denies anyone and is able and wants to heal everyone. What does it matter if it is not He who touches me, but I who touch Him? Just one touch to His clothing is enough for me, and even He Himself will not know about this. She made her way to Him through the crowd of people who pressed against Him and gently touched the hem of His garment. In that very moment, she was healed.

At first glance, it seems that she took her healing regardless of the wishes of Jesus, but this is just an illusion. She knew that Jesus wished to help everyone, so through touching His garment, it was as if she opened the door that allowed God's power to touch her body. Jesus had just felt that His strength had left Him, so He asked: "Who touched Me?" He knew that this touch was not just an ordinary touch, but a touch of faith; the kind of touch that received.

Every Christian, as God's heir, may exercise his right to be healed. As we accept forgiveness, we can receive healing as well. Forgiveness belongs to everyone who repents, and in this same way, healing belongs to everyone who believes.

James speaks of Christian treatments for the sick in his letter:

> Is anyone among you sick? Let him call for the elders of the church, and let them pray over him, anointing him with oil in the name of the Lord. And the prayer of faith will save the sick, and the Lord will raise him up. And if he has committed sins, he will be forgiven. Confess your trespasses to one another, and pray for one another, that you may be healed. The effective, fervent prayer of a righteous man avails much. (James 5:14–16)

Since we have already recognized our transgressions, and God forgave us, the only thing we have left is to do is to use anointing oil, pray, and be healed. Your healing already belongs to you. In the name of Jesus of Nazareth, accept it and be healed.

CHAPTER 17

Vision for Life

Vision is defined as the desires and plans of God's heart put into the heart of a person so that they can become that person's plans, thoughts, and life goals.

Jesus said, "Come to me, all you labor and are heavy laden, and I will give you rest. Take My yoke upon you and learn from Me, for I am gentle and lowly in heart, and you will find rest for your souls. For My yoke is easy and My burden is light" (Matt. 11:28–30).

Each and every person who has ever come to God has had heavy burdens and hardships. The Devil has weighed all people down with sins, offenses, curses, enslavement, and various other problems. People who are burdened are useless to God because they are under a foreign yoke and are fulfilling a foreign will. For this reason, God invites each person to come to Him so that He can free him or her from all burdens. Many of us have already experienced this freedom, but it is only half the deal.

It has been said that a holy place cannot remain empty. In this earthly life, a person can never be burden free. That's why God invites each person to trade his or her earthly cares for His yolk and His burden. These are the things that God has His heart set on—His plans, desires, and goals. Through this exchange of burdens, God frees the hearts of humankind. God's will becomes our will; God's plans become our plans; God's desires become our desires; and God's goals become our goals. God's yolk is easy, and His burden is light, so His will is pleasant and satisfying.

There are only two types of life: life in the flesh, and life in the will of God. To live in the flesh means to live according to the world, which is consumed with lust, and it also means living by the Devil's will.

> And you He made alive, who were dead in trespasses and sins, in which you once walked according to the course of this world, according to the prince of the power of the air, the spirit who now works in the sons of disobedience, among whom also we all once conducted ourselves in the lusts of our flesh, fulfilling the desires of the flesh and of the mind, and were by nature children of wrath, just as the others. (Eph. 2:1–3)

In fulfilling their lusts, many people think that they live for themselves, but the Bible says that they live by the will of the Devil. This kind of life does not bring pleasure, but instead leads to slavery and death.

The apostle Peter taught Christians: "Therefore, since Christ suffered for us in the flesh, arm yourselves also with the same mind, for he who has suffered in the flesh has ceased from sin, that he no longer should live the rest of his time in the flesh for the lusts of men, but for the will of God. For we have spent enough of our past lifetime in doing the will of the Gentiles ..." (1 Peter 4:1–3).

The apostle Peter says that we no longer have the right to live for our lusts and for ourselves. There is only one way to live, and that is to live by the will of God.

Jesus told His disciples, "If anyone desires to come after me, let him deny himself, and take up his cross, and follow me" (Matt. 16:24).

As sad as it is, each person was born on this earth as an egocentric individual. From the very day of our births, we are accustomed to being loved, served, and having someone else fulfill our desires. When a child is born on the earth, he or she becomes the center of attention; parents, brothers, and sisters encircle the child. When the child wants to eat, he or she lets out a siren-like signal, and they feed the child. When he or she is smelly in a certain place, the child lets out that same signal, and they change him or her. If the child is tired of sleeping, the signal fires, and he or she is instantly taken into someone's arms. The child is fed, clothed, bathed, nursed, and picked up after; all of this is good and proper. But the baby's mind has already created the illusion that he or she is the center of the family and that all should revolve around the child.

The child then grows up and learns about God. He or she comes to church, people smile at the child, invite him or her forward, bring the child home, and want to know how he or she feels. The child thinks, *Wow, this is great! The church is all about me, the pastor is for me, and even God is for me.*

The child comes to God with a list of requests and orders: "I need this," "Help me in that," "Keep me safe in this," and so on. At first, this is normal, but one day, the one who is really at the center will be revealed to the child, and the One around whom all does and should revolve will become known to him or her.

In ancient times, when there were still no telescopes, people looking at the heavenly lights came to the conclusion that the earth was the center of the solar system. Each day they saw the sun and the moon in a different relationship to the earth, and this seemed to confirm their theory. People lived for hundreds of years thinking this way, until the telescope was invented. Only then did the revelation come to them that the earth revolves around the sun and not the other way around. Understanding this reality helped them travel into outer space and launch multitudes of satellites that now work for humankind.

Every Christian should examine his or her heart to see who is truly at the center of his or her universe—that person or God. If that person is at the center, then God should serve him or her and fulfill all of that person's desires. If the center is God, then that person should live for Him and fulfill His desires. This revelation is the first step to a vision.

Only when a person's life takes on real meaning, and only when a person comes out of his or her own orbit, does that person begin to live entirely for God's grace, pleasure, and perfect will. That person no longer comes to prayer with a list of his or her requests, but with a clean sheet of paper to write down God's desires and instruction. This does not mean that the that person's desires are nullified, of course, but that he or she has learned to put them on the back burner for God.

What are God's plans and desires?

God's biggest desire, and around which all His plans revolve, is that all people would be saved and come to the knowledge of truth (1 Tim. 2:4). This is why He gave His Son, Jesus, to die a shameful death. For this purpose, the Holy Spirit came and gave gifts to humankind. This is the only reason that the earth still exists today.

The salvation of all is the biggest burden on the heart of the Father God. He desires to lay this same burden on the heart of every Christian. The greatest, most important commandment that Jesus left His faithful followers and friends with was to go into all the earth, preach the gospel, and make disciples.

"Go therefore and make disciples of all the nations, baptizing them in the name of the Father and of the Son and of the Holy Spirit, teaching them to observe all things that I have commanded you; and lo, I am with you always, even to the end of the age" (Matt. 28:19–20).

"And He said to them, 'Go into all the world and preach the gospel to every creature'" (Mark 16:15).

For this purpose He sent the Holy Spirit, so that with His help, this commandment can be fulfilled. "But you shall receive power when the Holy Spirit has come upon you; and you shall be witnesses to Me in Jerusalem, and in all Judea and Samaria, and to the end of the earth" (Acts 1:8).

When it is fulfilled, the end will come. "And this gospel of the kingdom will be preached in all the world as a witness to all the nations, and then the end will come" (Matt. 24:14).

We have already said that a true encounter with God always leaves an indelible mark on the heart of an individual. God always seals His own desires into a person, and this is the salvation of all people.

Moses experienced an unforgettable encounter with God at the burning bush. Since then, his life was never the same. He left his quiet and carefree life and went to rescue his people from slavery in Egypt. He devoted the rest of his life to the service of the people. Because of this, he saw and experienced tremendous power, miracles, and the revelation of God in his life. That's what made him the greatest hero in the eyes of God and hundreds of generations of people.

Isaiah saw God sitting on the throne, high and exalted. Having gone through conviction in his conscience, repentance, and the cleansing fire, he heard God's eternal question: "Whom shall I send, and who will go for Us?" (Isa. 6:8)

He answered with the following words: "Here am I! Send me" (Isa. 6:8).

He was sent to preach to the people and became the first preacher of the gospel living in era of the Old Testament. No one else spoke so much of the sacrifice of Jesus Christ and the riches it entailed as Isaiah did.

Saul met with the very One whom he chased and resisted. This meeting turned his inner being inside out and changed the course of his entire life. He became the great apostle Paul, who was sent to minister to the Gentiles. He preached to them, ministered to them, defended their freedom, and for their sake, he died.

Jesus said of Himself, "Just as the Son of Man did not come to be served, but to serve, and to give His life a ransom for many" (Matt. 20:28).

Parting with His disciples, He said, "As the Father has sent Me, I also send you" (John 20:21).

Every Christian is called to fulfill the will of God, minister to people, and if necessary, die for Him. The biggest desire of God, though, is that all people would be saved. Humankind, having experienced a real encounter with God, is ignited with that same passion to save people. A Christian can work a lot in the name and for the sake of God, but if he or she does not fulfill the main decree, then there is no use for his or her efforts.

God has a special place in His body for every saved person and has a calling for the implementation of His plan. For a Christian to move into his or her calling, the Christian first needs to find out what it is and accept it.

"I beseech you therefore, brethren, by the mercies of God, that you present your bodies a living sacrifice, holy, acceptable to God, which is your reasonable service. And do not be conformed to this world, but be transformed by the renewing of your mind, that you may prove what is that good and acceptable and perfect will of God" (Rom. 12:1–2)..

"For in fact the body is not one member but many. But now God has set the members, each one of them, in the body just as He pleased" (1 Cor. 12:14, 18).

After this, it is crucial to deny oneself and to take up one's cross: "If anyone desires to come after Me, let him deny himself, and take up his cross, and follow me" (Matt. 16:24).

The cross contains several important features:

Firstly, it helps keep our flesh, and our old natures, in a crucified state. Secondly, it helps us deny ourselves and obey the will of God. Thirdly, the cross represents two dimensions, vertical and horizontal. The vertical represents our relationship to heaven, and the horizontal our relationship to people.

To live the life of the cross means to seek a close, deep relationship with God daily. This relationship is built through faith and a childlike trust in God. It also requires prayer, obedience to Him, worship, and a deep study of His Word. All that Jesus did on the earth was done in the strength of the Holy Spirit. It is impossible to live for God without the Holy Spirit. For that reason, before a Christian leaves his or her prayer room, he or she needs to be filled with the Holy Spirit. Only then can the Christian serve those around him or her. A strong vertical relationship gives a person the ability to build healthy horizontal relationships.

Jesus said that His disciples would be witnesses in Jerusalem, in all of Judea, in Samaria, and to the ends of the earth. Our evangelism starts in our home, meaning our family. God ordained a special place for each person in the family, so each Christian should first of all take that proper place that God has ordained for him or her in his or her own home. Some people pray and say, "O Lord, send me to Africa," and God says, "Go home—that is your Africa." This is because some people's homes are truly like a jungle; they lack true relationships, love, and order.

The very first place where a man should bring the full gospel of God's kingdom is to his family. God made man the head, leader, manager, provider, pastor, priest, protector, gentle father, and loving husband for his family. The husband is responsible for every single thing that occurs in his home. He is responsible for finances, rearing the children, keeping order, cleanliness, housing, transportation, bills, washing, cleaning, and more. This doesn't mean that the man does this all by himself. It means that he answers to God for all of these things just as if God were the boss of his business. A good manager is not one who does everything himself, but one who can organize things well and delegate tasks to those assisting him. A man should be a light and an example to his wife and his children because he represents God in his home. As children perceive their father, so they form their impressions of God.

God made woman to be a loving and faithful wife who submits to her husband, as well as a gentle, caring mother who takes care of her children. She should understand the areas that her husband may need help in and serve him with joy. Through her kind conduct, she can captivate the heart of her husband, even the unbelieving husband, and without speaking about her faith, lead her husband to the Lord.

A good, friendly, and warm relationship between parents creates a favorable atmosphere to raise children. To be a witness in Jerusalem is to be a witness in one's own home, spreading God's love, gentleness, and goodness. The first people that we should bring to God are our children. This happens through the parents' personal example and by raising the children up in the gospel.

"Judea" represents your local church. Earlier I spoke about how when a person came to church, God had already appointed him or her a place in His body. He prepared a calling for the person and gave him or her a measure of faith to fulfill his or her ministry (Rom. 12). A calling has nothing in common with a dream. A calling is directly connected to the will of God, and it is something that a Christian must know and fulfill. God will judge our work on earth not on the basis of how busy we were but on how well we fulfilled His will in our lives.

Each person needs to become rooted in the local church and become a member in the body of Christ. Each person should offer his or her body to the Holy Spirit as a living sacrifice for service to God. A person should be so rooted in the church that if he or she moves to a different city, the church should truly feel that it has lost someone important and needed. In church, a person should love his or her brothers, be friendly, sacrificial, and social. A person should serve others with all the gifts that he or she has received from God.

"Samaria" represents the place that one lives, works, or studies and the circle of people that he or she interacts with. God has appointed us to be light and salt where we are found. It is precisely through us that God wants to reveal His love and the message of the gospel to others.

The whole earth lives in evil, lies, and depravity. Only those who are saved know what true happiness is. Only we know of salvation and true freedom. Therefore, we are responsible before God for each person who we meet each day. No one can tell them of salvation except us, the ones who are saved.

There are so many broken families, destroyed destinies, and crippled lives today. People are trapped in the dead ends that they have created for themselves. They have no idea that the days they spend on this earth without God will lead them to forever walk in darkness where there will be weeping and gnashing of teeth. We will answer before God for all the people that He has allowed us to meet.

Our calling is to be good Samaritans to all those who are wounded by sin and the Devil. Only after we accomplish this can we go to the ends of the earth. Only when we have achieved faithfulness in our families, served people in the church, and brought love and warmth to those around us will we be free to bring the gospel to the entire world.

Today, God has men and women who have stopped living for themselves, who are not looking out for their own rights, who have left behind their ambitions and completely consecrated themselves to the service of God and people. There is very little time left, and the work that needs to be done is very great. As in the past, today a voice is crying out from heaven: "Whom shall I send? And who will go for Us?" (Isa. 6:8).

Who is ready to fully present him- or herself to God today? Who agrees to accept the burden that God has on His heart? Each and every one of us can be that person.

One day, a missionary who was located in a faraway foreign country experienced an inner struggle. His life was threatened by a deadly danger. He was in a place of serious struggle and didn't know which way to go. To remain in the country meant to agree to death. To leave it meant to give up and neglect his duty. On the morning following this struggle, he was found murdered in his home. On the table was found a piece of paper where he had written down the decision he had made.

Consecration

- ❏ I am one of those who have firmly decided to be true to the end.
- ❏ I have stepped over the boundary and have made a decision: I am a disciple of Jesus Christ.
- ❏ I refuse the things of the earth for the sake of knowing Him.
- ❏ I have the authority of Jesus Christ and the strength of the Holy Spirit.
- ❏ Obeying Jesus Christ and His Word, I will not look back, grow weary, slow down, or turn back.
- ❏ My past is redeemed, my present makes sense, and my future is safe.
- ❏ I have forever finished living a fruitless life, walking the fence, making insignificant plans, seeing with distorted vision, engaging in empty speech, participating in boring activities, and setting vague goals.
- ❏ I am one of those who have firmly decided to persevere to the end.

- ❏ I no longer need glory.
- ❏ I am no longer interested in circumstances.
- ❏ I no longer need to be popular.
- ❏ I don't have to be right.
- ❏ I don't have to be first.
- ❏ I don't have to be on top.
- ❏ I am not dependent on calling and respect; I don't expect to be praised by people and am not looking for a reward.
- ❏ I live in God's presence now. I hold on to faith.
- ❏ I love patience. I live in prayer and apply myself diligently.
- ❏ I am one of those who have firmly decided to persevere to the end.
- ❏ I forge ahead, my vision is firm, and my goal is heaven.
- ❏ My way is narrow and straight, but my leader is trustworthy, and my mission is clear.
- ❏ You cannot buy me, make me compromise, turn me back, or deceive me. You can't make me turn back or lead me astray. I do not tremble at the necessity of sacrificing myself, and I will not doubt when the hard times come. I will not sit down at the table and converse with the Enemy.
- ❏ I will not give up, keep silent, or grow weak until I have finished preaching. I will not stop praying until I have paid the price, gathered the whole harvest, and stood with Christ to the very end.

- ❏ Until the return of Jesus Christ, I will continue to move forward, preach while people still do not know Him, and work as long as He allows me.
- ❏ And when God comes to take His children home, it will be easy for Him to recognize me because I have consecrated my life to be among those who have firmly decided to persevere to the end.

Each of us can be among those who have firmly decided to persevere with Christ until the end. Shouldn't you be among those people?

Recommended Reading

- Horrobin Peter. Healing throw deliverance 1. Sovereign World, Ltd. (May 1991)
- Horrobin Peter. Healing throw deliverance 2. Sovereign World, Ltd. (October 1992)
- Virkler Mark and Patti. Prayers That Heal the Hearts. Bridge-Logos Publishers (Jan 2001)
- Prince Derek. They Shall Expel Demons. Chosen Books; Reprinted edition (May 1, 1998)
- Bevere John. Bait of Satan. Charisma House; Revised edition (June 1, 2004)
- Frost Jack. Experiencing Father's Embrace. Father's House Productions; 2 edition (2002)
- Malone Henry. Shadow Boxing. Father's House Productions; 2 edition (2002)
- School of Deliverance. http://www.impactdeliverancecenter.org.

You can contact the author
and order the book
using the following information:

healingofthesoul55@yahoo.com
www.healingofthesoul.org

www.ingramcontent.com/pod-product-compliance
Lightning Source LLC
Chambersburg PA
CBHW041625140626
46547CB00030B/887